Heavenly

Worship

Releasing Your Spirit to Faith, Hope and Destiny

Peter Todd

DESTINY IMAGE EUROPE
Via Maiella, 1
66020 San Giovanni Teatino (Ch) - Italy

ISBN: 88-89127-12-0

For Worldwide Distribution
Printed in the U.S.A.

1 2 3 4 5 6 7 8/10 09 08 07 06 05

This book and all other Destiny Image Europe books are available at Christian bookstores and distributors worldwide.

To order products, or for any other correspondence:

DESTINY IMAGE EUROPE
Via Acquacorrente, 6
65123 - Pescara - Italy
Tel. +39 085 4716623 - Fax: +39 085 4716622
E-mail: info@eurodestinyimage.com

Or reach us on the Internet:
www.eurodestinyimage.com

Dedication

To Julia, my loving wife,

Whom God has used

More than anyone else

To show me His gracious kindness,

His steadfast faithfulness,

And His unfailing love

With all my love,

Peter

Valentine's Day 2005

Acknowledgements

꧁ꕥ꧂

Many people have contributed to the completion of this book. First, and preeminently, I am grateful to God. For years, I did not venture to preach out of certain passages of Scripture, as they seemed to be beyond my ability to comprehend. The Book of Revelation was one such book. However, over the course of a few months, God began to open my eyes to see what I had not been able to see before. He used the work of other authors, friends from our church community, and my wife and children in this process. I am very grateful for all that He has taught me through them. He loves to reveal Himself to His children, and I am eternally thankful for every bit of revelation that He has ever given me.

After I overcame my nervousness of preaching on the Book of Revelation, chapters 4 and 5, someone suggested that I should put these sermons into book form. I am grateful to all those who encouraged me in this endeavor, and there were many who did. I especially thank the elders and people of Gateway Christian Community (particularly the south congregation), who supported me over the last ten years and believed in me enough to release me to a short sabbatical during which much of this manuscript was written.

I have had the special privilege of growing and maturing in ministry under the kind pastoral care and leadership of Ron MacLean.

Along with Barney Coombs, he has done more than anyone to help me sharpen and hone my God-given gifts. I am very grateful to the Lord for bringing both these fine men of God into my life. I am also very grateful to Fiona Peters, who did an excellent job of reviewing and editing the manuscript. Without her thorough and professional help, I would not have been able to complete this book.

I was brought up with a rich heritage in music and worship. My parents and grandparents are all worshipers, and I owe them a huge debt of gratitude for the inheritance that they have given me. In turn, the Lord has given four precious girls to Julia and I. They have brought tremendous joy and happiness into my life. In different ways, God has used each one of them to teach me about Himself. Whenever I think of them, I am moved by how richly God has blessed me.

Above all others in this world, I am deeply grateful to my wife, Julia. She has loved, supported, and encouraged me through good times and bad. She challenges me and provokes me into greater joy and fruitfulness. She has believed in what God has given me when I have been unable to believe myself. She has given of herself, many times sacrificially, to see me flourish in becoming all that God has made me to be. Her selfless love and servant heart have been a constant inspiration to me. Without her, this book would not have been written. I am deeply grateful to God for giving me such a wonderful wife.

Contents

Foreword

For over 40 years, I have had a great interest in praise and worship. I have read many books and articles in Christian magazines relating to the subject. As a preacher, I have endured more than my fair share of worship leaders manipulating God's people into producing a better effort. God has put a longing in everyone's heart to be a worshiper. It is a universal desire! Those who fail to discover God to be the supreme focus of love will seek other outlets to quench that thirst, but will always remain unfulfilled and dissatisfied. *Heavenly Worship* is probably the best book I have ever read on the subject.

Peter Todd is a songwriter with special anointing. He is a gifted musician, worship leader, and pastor. He is also a special friend. As you read this book, you will find your heart being effortlessly drawn toward God's throne. This is not a "doing" book that promotes methods and techniques. *Heavenly Worship* is a "being" book, whereby you find yourself drinking from the fountain of living water and experiencing rivers of love and joy springing forth. At times, all you can give yourself to is silent contemplation on Christ Himself. What gets pumped up by human effort will never suffice. Only that which comes down from Heaven above will please God and bring deep satisfaction to your soul. My prayer is that Heavenly Worship will have a wide circulation—because the church of Jesus Christ needs it.

Barney Coombs
Salt and Light Ministries

Meet the Author

Peter Todd grew up in northern England. As the son of a school principal and pastor, Peter was raised in a rich Christian heritage and he developed a deep love for the Word of God. He completed a degree in music at the University of Hull, and then graduated with teaching credentials from the University of Durham. He began his career as a teaching instructor in Gateshead.

In 1992, Peter sensed a strong leading from God to leave his homeland and go to Winnipeg, Canada. He gave up a successful teaching position and volunteered in our Christian school for two years. His teaching expertise, musical skill, and shepherd's heart were of incredible value. During these years, Peter reconnected with his long-time friend Julia Elderton, who at that time was living and working in China. Julia also made the journey to Canada, and they were married on Christmas Day 1994. Since then, they have been blessed with four beautiful daughters.

In 1995, our church planted another congregation, and it became clear that Peter should be the pastor of this new work. Under his leadership these past nine years, the church has grown and prospered. His skillful leadership and heart of worship have significantly impacted the life and direction of the entire Gateway Christian Community.

Peter is an extraordinary servant of the Lord with an extraordinary revelation of worship. He is both a worshiper and a warrior; he is a prayer and a preacher; and he is a songwriter and an author. He "sees" with prophetic passion and insight, and he "oversees" with pastoral wisdom and tenderness. He is a true spiritual son and friend.

What this book is all about is the worship of Heaven. Peter has been an immeasurable blessing to me personally, and to our church community and city. I trust that he will also be a blessing to you, as you read this book. May this revelation of Heaven's worship of the Lamb of God saturate your soul and give you a passion to spread Jesus' fame among the nations.

Ron MacLean
Pastor, Gateway Christian Community
Winnipeg, Canada
January 2005

Introduction

On the last Sunday of December 2000, I preached a message based on the first two chapters of the Gospel of Luke. My message was supposed to be a stand-alone sermon, not part of a series. However, I had no idea of the impact that this sermon would have on me personally and on our congregation.

When studying these passages, I was struck by the manner in which Luke had constructed his account; it focused on people and their remarkable encounters with God. The lives of ordinary people were broken into supernaturally as God revealed Himself to them. What particularly caught my attention, however, were not the encounters themselves, but people's response to them. Luke seemed to be highlighting a pattern that he wanted his readers to grasp.

The verse that jumped out at me the most was Luke 1:64, which says of Zechariah that *"immediately his mouth was opened and his tongue was loosed."* As I looked at the other God-encounters in these two chapters, I noticed the same occurrence in each case. God supernaturally revealed Himself and something of His purpose, and the result was the loosening of tongues in worship and witness. Luke highlights four responses to these revelations: Zechariah's, the shepherds', Simeon's, and Anna's.

Simeon and Anna were quite similar: Simeon was a God-seeker while Anna was devoted to fervent prayer and worship. Both were living in faith for the coming of God. You would expect that God would want to reveal Himself to such people. Zechariah was an "upright" man and a "blameless" priest, but he seemed to have little faith for what God was about to do. That lack of belief, however, was not reason enough for God to exclude him from His plans. So, he too was given a personal and glorious revelation.

The shepherds came from an altogether different walk of life. Out in the field trying to eke out a living, they are not described as having any connection with God at all. They are simply *"shepherds living out in the fields nearby, keeping watch over their flocks at night"* (Luke 2:8). They were probably not waiting for much more than their next meal and a better place to sleep. However, God chose to move on them as well.

God revealed Himself to each of them, as they were going about their usual business. All responded in the same way: with spontaneous, thankful praise and worship. In the case of Zechariah and Simeon, the worship overflowed into wonderful prophetic declarations. Zechariah, Anna, and the shepherds were loosed into powerful witness. The shepherds—who lacked the training and preparation of Zechariah and Anna—were every bit as effective in spreading the good news: *"and all who heard it were amazed at what the shepherds said to them"* (Luke 2:18). After all, they had also seen the King. The revelation they received made them effective evangelists and worshipers.

The words that flowed from these people had an extraordinary impact on the entire surrounding area: *"The neighbors were all filled with awe, and throughout the hill country of Judea people were talking about these things. Everyone who heard this wondered about it, asking, 'What then is this child going to be?'"* (Luke 1:65-66). God had moved in! He touched those with lives characterized by fervent waiting and longing, and He also touched those just going about ordinary business. He revealed Himself in wonderful, supernatural ways and, as a result, tongues were loosened in worship and witness. Then, the whole area became alive with gossip about the good news. Luke records a similar outbreak of God-awareness that took place 33 years later when the Holy Spirit loosed tongues of those in the upper room so they could preach the gospel (see Acts 2).

The pattern seemed to be clear. Revelation of God leads to greater worship and witness. While meditating on the joy and zeal of the people highlighted by Luke, I realized that I needed a fresh vision of God myself. For Christmas, I had been given a calendar that included a picture of Simeon holding the baby Jesus in his arms; the Holy Spirit had moved him to this place of revelation. The tears in Simeon's upturned eyes revealed the glorious broken-ness brought about by such wonderful kindness. God will allow us to see and touch that which our hearts most long for—He will allow us to see and touch Himself!

A few weeks earlier, I had just completed a series on First John. The writer begins the letter by talking about *"that which was from the beginning, which we have heard, which we have seen with our eyes, which we have looked at and our hands have touched..."* (1 John 1:1). The progression was striking. In my mind's eye, I could see an ordinary Galilean who had heard stories about this amazing teacher and miracle worker called Jesus. His curiosity is aroused, so he goes out to join the crowds.

There is a "buzz" about the atmosphere and a little group appears. Jesus is among them and He starts to speak—"that which we have heard." Drawn by the grace and truth that he hears, the man moves closer to get a better look—"that which we have seen with our eyes." The words he heard excited his curiosity, but now he can see and becomes captivated. He finds himself staring—"that which we have looked at."

It all becomes too much to bear—something within him breaks and he pushes his way to the front. What he heard was interesting and what he saw was captivating, but the longer he looked, the more he was overcome by one compelling desire. Hearing, seeing, and gazing weren't enough; he had to be close and had to touch Him—"that which...our hands have touched."

That progression at the beginning of John's letter is what encourages us to push forward into deeper levels of intimacy with God. If we have only heard, let us ask that we may see. If we have seen, let us ask for opportunity to look at, *"to gaze upon the beauty of the Lord,"* as noted in Psalm 27:4. If we have been allowed to gaze, that is glorious in itself, but there is still more. Let us press in to touch Him.

Simeon had touched Him! The artist who illustrated my calendar so vividly caught the life-changing joy of that moment by showing Simeon's tear-filled eyes and posture towards Heaven. "Lord," I prayed, "that's what I need! I want to see You like that. I want to touch You! I want a whole new revelation of who You are, so that my tongue may be loosed into worship and witness in such a way that You are glorified and many people are touched."

The good news—for both Christian and non-Christian—is that a fresh revelation of God is possible because, in Christ, the veil that hides Him from us is taken away. *"But whenever anyone turns to the Lord, the veil is taken away"* (2 Cor. 3:16). Furthermore, we are meant to gaze upon the beauty and glory of God, so that we can reflect it to others around us. *"And we, who with unveiled faces all reflect the Lord's glory, are being transformed into His likeness with ever increasing glory, which comes from the Lord, who is the Spirit"* (2 Cor. 3:18).

I have asked myself, "How much glory do I reflect?" If I reflect so little, then it must be because I do so little gazing into God Himself. My eyes must be focused elsewhere. When I realized my poverty of spirit, I cried out to the Lord for help. What is wonderful is that the Lord has helped us! He gave us the Bible to help us see, look, and gaze upon the glory of God. With the wise counsel and teaching of the Holy Spirit, our eyes can be opened—even if, at first, we see only blurred images, like those of a newborn child.

In answer to a growing hunger for a fresh encounter with God, I was led to the Book of Revelation, particularly the fourth and fifth chapters. Here, we are presented with *"a door standing open in heaven"* (Rev. 4:1). This is not just a window into Heaven—through which we only catch a distant glimpse—but it is a door. We can walk through and approach this entrance because the invitation is there for us to "come up," to draw near.

As a church, we spent the first few months of 2001 in study and meditation of these chapters. These were rich times for us. In the hope that others would also be blessed, I was encouraged to put these sermons into book form. My prayer is that the Holy Spirit would use Heavenly Worship to refresh and renew your vision of God. Hopefully, these words will give you opportunity to hold that vision in your hands, like Simeon, and gaze into the intense beauty and majesty set before you. Perhaps your heart will be stirred once again by a noble theme, and you will overflow in joyful worship and witness for His glory.

CHAPTER 1

The Fuel of Heavenly Worship

The Need for Eye Salve

Before we enter the wonders of Revelation 4 and 5, let's look at a little key at the end of Revelation 3, which can help unlock the door into treasures of the next two chapters. That key has to do with our eyes. If our eyes are open, then we will be able to see into Heaven itself. But, are our eyes open? Maybe our eyes are like those of the Laodicean church.

As Eugene Peterson points out in his book, *Reversed Thunder: The Revelation of St. John and the Praying Imagination*, the Church sits in between the two great revelations of Christ in the Book of Revelation, chapters 1 and 4. What exists here are reviews of the seven churches. (The Holy Spirit has preserved Paul's letters to these seven churches, and they may contain a message for the universal Church, as there is in his epistles.) The seven reviews are remarkable for their brevity, but apparently that is all that needs to be said to each congregation.

In order to go from the glory of the first vision of Christ to the greater glory of Revelation 4, you have to go through the Church; and it's not a church in all its splendor but one of ordinariness, with a seemingly equal number of triumphs and troubles. *"It is not possible to have Christ apart from the church"* (*Reversed Thunder*, Chapter

Four). Again, as Peterson explains, even though this same church later appears as the Bride of Christ and the New Jerusalem, Jesus is already "in the midst," despite her obvious inadequacies. God does not seem concerned about placing His glory in clay vessels (see 2 Cor. 4:7).

When we talk of inadequacies, the last church—Laodicea—seems to have had the most. *"Wretched, pitiful, poor, blind and naked"* (Rev. 3:17) is quite a review, particularly when—unlike every other church Christ looks at—He can find nothing good to say about them! This does not seem like a good place in which to find keys to a greater life with God. Neither does it appear to be a helpful springboard into the heavenly realms described in Revelation 4.

Thankfully, the Lord of our Church is not finished with the weakest, most lukewarm member of His Body. Jesus gives them guidance on to how to move forward. He counsels them to *"buy...gold refined in the fire...white clothes to wear, so you can cover your shameful nakedness; and salve to put on your eyes, so you can see"* (Rev. 3:18). Suddenly, within six verses, we are nearer to God than we have ever been before.

The congregation of Laodicea must have been quite shocked to listen to this prophecy. Having heard what Jesus said to the other churches, they must have been thoroughly discouraged by the time their own review was read! However, before they had a chance to digest it all, they were transported into Heaven itself. The contrast is stunning, but it is a wonderful encouragement to all of us who get overwhelmed by day-to-day troubles of the Church.

Glory is available to us, if we desire it—even in the most discouraging of situations, when we are face-to-face with full implications of our own failures. To this, the most pitiful of the seven churches, Christ gives the most awesome encouragement: *"To him who overcomes, I will give the right to sit with Me on My throne..."* (Rev. 3:21a). We can choose where we want to live! Jesus graciously asks for entrance into the Laodicean church by knocking on their closed door (see Rev. 3:20). All the while, His own door—the gateway to Heaven—stands permanently open as an invitation for them to "come up" and be with Him.

The letter's first reading in Laodicea must have caused some disquiet among the listening congregation. I can imagine someone jumping up at the beginning of Revelation 4 and interrupting the reader: "Hold on a minute! We can't just suddenly move on. Listen to what Jesus has just said. We can't just change gear and suddenly start thinking about Heaven—we need to sort out our own mess first! Didn't Jesus say anything more to John? We must have lost some pages!" The reader would have had to reply, "No, there's nothing more said about us—it just abruptly moves heavenward."

Moving toward Heaven is the best move to make after a receiving bad review. The answers to our earthly problems are not to be found in the physical realm, but only before the throne of Almighty God. Is our mind focused on earth or Heaven? Are we more likely to focus on the reality of present difficulties surrounding us, or on the greater reality of God's glory that surrounds all our difficulties?

Jesus obviously felt that the seven churches needed both. A quick dose of reality was needed to prevent them from living in deception or discouragement; but they also needed to be swiftly carried away by the Spirit into an incredible, life-changing view of Heaven's landscape. The result would be a whole new perspective on life: God is on the throne; the Lamb has triumphed; the victory is secured; the end is in sight, and it is absolutely glorious!

Some Christians have been accused of being so heavenly minded that they are no earthly use. It could be equally said, however, that many of us have become so earthly minded, that we are of little heavenly use! A view into Heaven is a wonderful tonic for a heavy heart, and it can keep us pushing through all sorts of difficulties. Paul understood this principle, so he encouraged the Colossian church to *"set your hearts on things above, where Christ is seated at the right hand of God. Set your minds on things above, not on earthly things"* (Col. 3:1-2).

How do we see afresh into Heaven? A good place to start would be to examine what Jesus offered the Laodiceans to give them the opportunity to stop looking at their problems and instead gaze into Heaven itself. One element offered by Jesus was eye salve, "so you can see."

The Need to Buy Eye Salve

In the fall of 2000, I had the privilege of listening to DeVern Fromke, the writer of such books as *Unto Full Stature* and *The Ultimate Intention*. He began one of his talks by saying, "You understand that there are some things that come to us freely by grace and there are some things that need to be bought." He then opened up the Scripture to Revelation 3:18: *"I counsel you to buy from Me gold refined in the fire, so you can become rich; and white clothes to wear, so you can cover your shameful nakedness; and salve to put on your eyes, so you can see."* Much of what I say here about eye salve comes from his talk on that powerful, life-changing evening.

What Jesus offered to the Laodicean church had to be bought from Him! As DeVern Fromke pointed out, this is not the new eyesight received when one first comes to understand the truth. When the enemy's blinders are removed, that new vision is freely received by sovereign, undeserved grace. No, this eye salve must be bought as we go through our Christian lives, particularly if we are becoming lukewarm. This is not "works"; it appears to be part of the continuing work of sanctifying grace in our lives, and that requires our willing participation.

Jesus has already told the Church that it is "blind," even though, at one time, it must have seen clearly enough to get saved. Obviously, over time, its eyesight had not improved but had, in fact, diminished. In Matthew 6:22, Jesus had already warned His disciples against this happening to them. *"The eye is the lamp of the body. If your eyes are good, your whole body will be full of light. But if your eyes are bad, your whole body will be full of darkness. If then the light within you is darkness, how great is that darkness!"*

Eye salve is given to help us see more clearly what needs to be seen, and it washes away obstructions and impediments to our eyesight. The eyes of the Laodicean church members were no longer good. In fact, they had become so full of darkness that they were diagnosed as blind. Thankfully, Jesus—the Light of the World— loves to make blind eyes see! So, He counsels them to come to Him and buy this eye salve.

What Is Eye Salve?

Scripture has many examples of people who seemed to possess what Jesus was talking about; one such person would be Simeon. Year after year, many babies passed through the temple courts, and Simeon had been waiting and watching for a long time. When Mary and Joseph appeared with their firstborn, they would have looked no different than any other poor couple, at least to the untrained eye! But Simeon's eye had been trained by years of waiting, and he saw in this little child what no one else saw. He had eye salve!

As Jesus came to Jericho, a large crowd was gathered around Him. Many of them, I am sure, were pushing for a better look. They had seen miracles, had heard His teachings, and were enamored with what they had witnessed. Despite all that evidence presented to their natural senses, the blind man, Bartimaeus, is the one who saw most clearly. He called Jesus by His messianic title—*"Son of David"*—and proved that although his physical sight was fully dark, light still did shine in his spiritual eyes (see Mark 10:47). Jesus could have said to him as He said to Peter, *"flesh and blood did not reveal this to you, but My Father who is in heaven..."* (Matt. 16:17 NAS). When Bartimaeus was asked by Jesus, *"What do you want Me to do for you?"* he replied, *"Rabbi, I want to see"* (Mark 10:51). But, spiritually, the blind man already had excellent sight because he had eye salve.

In 1820, a baby girl was born to a Puritan family in the United States. After a few weeks, she developed an infection that inflamed her eyes. As good Puritans, the family probably prayed, but the village doctor was away. Unfortunately, the stand-in doctor put hot poultices on her eyes, which burnt her corneas and eliminated all her sight.

Despite this severe handicap, she grew up to become a musician, poet, and missionary to the poor. She was a friend of presidents and the first woman ever to address Congress. She also wrote many well-known hymns—including "Blessed Assurance" and "To God Be the Glory"—that have been sung worldwide and fueled great evangelistic works like those of D.L. Moody and Billy Graham. Moody was said to have credited her hymns with bringing more people to salvation than his sermons. Of her handicap, this woman wrote the following words:

> "I believe that the greatest blessing the Creator ever bestowed upon me was when He permitted my external vision to be closed. He consecrated me for the work for which He created me. I have never known what it is to see, and therefore cannot realize my personal loss. But I have had the most remarkable dreams; I have seen the prettiest eyes, the most beautiful faces, the most remarkable landscapes. The loss of sight has been no loss to me.... Sightless I see and seeing, find soul-vision, though my eyes are blind."

This woman, Fanny Crosby, had eye salve.

One of the tales I grew up with dealt with a preacher who came to my grandmother's home when she was a little girl. He was an uneducated man who made his living as a stonemason. In the evenings, he would preach the gospel in the local chapel to all who would listen. After a hard day working over the moors and fells of Cumberland, he would sit down before the fire and seemingly go to sleep. He would be aroused from his "slumber" in time to attend the meeting. Often, he would often look up and say a phrase like, "The Lord has given me four tonight!" Sure enough, that evening four people would get saved. The stonemason had eye salve. Like others before and after him, he saw beyond the natural world and his senses were alive to spiritual reality.

So, eye salve seems to represent the gift of revelation. It involves God washing away any impediments that stop us from clearly seeing what is of Heaven and eternity. It may only happen in a moment in time, but once our eyes are opened to a revelation from God, the truth seen will always be with us. As my friend Barney Coombs is fond of saying, "Once you have seen it, you will never forget it."

How Do We Get Eye Salve?

The questions are, "How do we get this eye salve?" and "Where do we buy it from?" The answer we are given by Jesus is, "You buy it from Me!" There is no explanation in Revelation 3 of how it works, or what we can do to increase our spiritual sight; all that we are told is that it is found in Jesus, who is the Light of the World.

Clues can be found in other parts of Scripture. Psalm 97:11 says, *"Light is shed upon the righteous...."* Luke describes Simeon as being a "righteous and devout" man. Isaiah 58:8 proclaims that light will "break forth like the dawn" for those who feed the hungry, shelter the poor, clothe the naked, and so on. Fanny Crosby would certainly fall into that category.

In Matthew 11:25-26, Jesus says, *"I praise You, Father, Lord of heaven and earth, because You have hidden these things from the wise and learned, and revealed them to little children. Yes, Father, for this was Your good pleasure."* A childlike heart sees clearer. Many an uneducated man—even a beggar like Bartimaeus or a humble stonemason—has had much better spiritual eyesight than those who are seen as more educated in the world's eyes.

Sometimes, the simplest principles are the ones most easily missed. Simeon saw the Messiah when others didn't, because he was looking for Him. No, not only was Simeon "looking," he was "waiting" in anticipation and eager expectation. Apparently, years of disappointment had not diminished his hope. His persevering faith was wonderfully rewarded, as it always is!

The writer of Hebrews encourages us to *"not throw away your confidence; it will be richly rewarded"* (Heb. 10:35). I like the word *richly*—it speaks of an intense and warm satisfaction that awaits those, like Simeon, who do not give up. The same writer then explains the reason for our hope: *"...anyone who comes to Him must believe that He exists and that He rewards those who earnestly seek Him"* (Heb. 11:6). If we want to see more of God, we need to have faith enough to look for Him!

The starting point in our quest for eye salve is obviously to go to Jesus and ask Him for it, even if we may have to pay for it! We can also ask for it on behalf of others, and not just ourselves. Paul prayed for the Ephesian church, *"I pray also that the eyes of your heart may be enlightened in order that you may know..."* (Eph. 1:18).

How Much Does Eye Salve Cost?

After having asked for eye salve, the truly difficult part may be in paying for it. For Fanny Crosby, it meant humbly embracing the process that God took her on when He allowed her sight to be lost. I am sure that many times she had to receive and participate with the grace that God made available to her in Christ. How else could she not become offended with the God that her parents had prayed to, and also forgive those who had hurt her. Beyond that, God's grace enabled Fanny to find purpose in the infirmity that her heavenly Father allowed her to carry.

Bartimaeus also had to actively participate when the grace of God was made available to him. Yes, Jesus did come near to him, but Bartimaeus had to push past ridicule and opposition to get a truer glimpse of the One he already saw in his heart. In his desperate pursuit of Jesus, Bartimaeus threw off his old identity and risked everything on the mercy of the Son of David.

As a personal testimony, when I ask for more eye salve, I find that I am crying soon afterwards. In the natural realm, tears are windshield washer fluid for our eyes, and they take away accumulated dust and irritations. For myself, I believe that tears are often a sign of my heart being cleansed. Pain, heaviness, and disappointments can easily accumulate in day-to-day life. If left unwashed, these begin to harden into sin in our hearts. Discouragement, unbelief, bitterness, and joylessness begin to turn what was light into darkness. Then, the eyes are no longer good!

But the love of God can come and begin to soften our hearts. It's sometimes evident in the flow of real tears that, suddenly, we begin to see clearer again. Jesus said, *"Blessed are the pure in heart, for they shall see God"* (Matt. 5:8). In each of these examples, the key to greater spiritual sight must be the work of the Holy Spirit. The Spirit of God leads us into all truth and He reveals God to us.

Paul connects the Spirit with eye salve in his prayer for the Ephesians, part of which I have already quoted. *"I keep asking that the God of our Lord Jesus Christ, the glorious Father, may give you the Spirit of wisdom and revelation, so that you may know Him better. I pray also that the eyes of your heart may be enlightened in order that you may know..."* (Eph. 1:17-18).

A prayer for more eye salve is also a request for more of the Holy Spirit; and that is one request that the Father loves to grant. *"If you then, though you are evil, know how to give good gifts to your children, how much more will your Father in heaven give the Holy Spirit to those that ask Him"* (Luke 11:13). The Spirit of God opens our eyes to see and understand more of God's Word. Therefore, it opens our hearts to receive more of God's glory. Implied in that statement is the absolute necessity for Christians to be reading Scripture with enabling and counsel from the Holy Spirit, and, therefore, to grow in revelation of the God being worshiped.

The encouragement to ask for eye salve needs to come with a caution. When our eyes are opened to spiritual reality in a greater way, we might not always enjoy the view! Obviously, the main reasons that the Laodiceans needed eye salve was to have their eyes opened to the reality of their own spiritual state—which was not a pretty sight! After asking for eye salve, we may have to face some uncomfortable realities about our spiritual stature here on earth before we are able to enjoy a fresh view of Heaven. However, those uncomfortable realities are not meant to disqualify us from seeing more of God's glory. In fact, they can be a springboard into His presence, if we respond correctly to them.

So, ask for eye salve. If you then start to become aware of hardness and coldness in your own heart, don't despair and retreat from the process. Instead, acknowledge the truth of what you are seeing, and then open the door for Jesus to enter those hard and cold places. You may be well surprised at how quickly Heaven opens up for you! When you get some revelation, then ask for more. John's eyes were opened progressively; five times in the Book of Revelation does he report his eyes being opened to new sights (see Rev. 4:1; 6:8; 14:1,14; and 15:5).

From Luke's narrative in the first two chapters of his Gospel, we can conclude that revelation of God is the fuel of worship and witness. The great hymn writer John Newton understood this principle. In his hymn, "How Sweet the Name of Jesus Sounds," he wrote the following verse:

Weak is the effort of my heart,

And cold my warmest thought,

But when I see Thee as Thou art

I'll praise Thee as I ought.

When our eyes are opened, we see what hasn't been seen before. In Revelation 4, what is seen right away is an open door to Heaven. This is a remarkable change in landscape from the bleakness of the Laodicean church, but perhaps it is only one dose of eye salve away!

CHAPTER 2

The Place of Heavenly Worship

Open Eyes, an Open Door, and an Open Heaven

The Laodicean church needed eye salve. New programs and a fresh set of goals do have their place, but this church needed to be transported out of its situation to spend some time viewing God's majesty and wonder. A change of landscape was necessary, and it had to be to a scene that would re-ignite a fire that was burning dangerously low.

"After this," said John, *"I saw..."* (Rev. 4:1). Eye salve will open your eyes. What John saw was designed specifically to fan the flame of the early Church's flickering lights. The reading of this prophecy would have stirred many to press on past obstacles of discouragement and persecution: *"...and there before me was a door standing open in heaven"* (Rev. 4:1).

Looking back again at Jesus' last review (in Rev. 3:20), He had said to the Church: *"Here I am!"* Just after His telling them that, they are close to being cast away from Him (see Rev. 3:16). In three simple but wonderful words, He explains that He hasn't left yet. He is still within reach—only their eyes have to be open to see Him!

He then continued: *"I stand at the door and knock"* (Rev. 3:20). Jesus was outside and wanted to be in, and He wanted to fellowship with

His people. If any one person in that congregation was willing to open the door, Jesus would eagerly accept the invitation: *"If anyone hears My voice and opens the door, I will come in..."* (Rev. 3:20). He would "eat with him" personally, regardless of where the rest of the Church was. Here is a wonderful promise: Even in the most lukewarm of congregations, it is still possible for an individual to invite Jesus to come and meet with him or her, and He will come.

However, for the time being, the door to the Laodicean church was shut. In contrast, a few verses later, we see a door standing open. The point is this: The door to the congregation may be closed to Jesus, but the door into Heaven is open for us! It doesn't need to be knocked on or pushed against. You don't need a certain amount of money or the correct password to get in. It is standing open! The literal translation is: "...having been opened." In other words, it was closed, but Christ's work on the Cross opened the door, and it has not been shut since. The veil has been torn in two, and whatever kept us out of God's manifest presence has been done away with.

It must be emphasized a *door* is standing open, not a window. We are not invited to sneak a look from a distance; we are invited to come right into the throne room of God Almighty and to make our home here in His presence! Jesus is saying, "I've opened My home to you. Will you open your home to Me?"

The Voice That Moves Us

Once again, John hears the voice that first ushered him into this vision, and that voice sounded like a trumpet. The first time he heard it (see Rev. 1:10), the voice came from behind him, and turned him around to see the true state of churches being carried in His heart. Such a view is necessary to any in church leadership, but it can also be quite disheartening. The wonderful encouragement here is that Jesus—the Lord of the Church—is not distant but *"among the lampstands..."* (see Rev. 1:13). Now, however, the voice comes not from behind, but from above: *"Come up here"* (Rev. 4:1). Instead of turning him around, this time it lifts his gaze upward to see the true state of Heaven, and Jesus is again in the midst (see Rev. 5:6).

I have often marveled at the intensely reverent, almost detached way, that John talks about Jesus. He refers to Him in his Gospel and letters by using such titles as "The Word" or "The Life." If anyone could call Jesus a "bosom buddy" or "best friend," it was John. He was the disciple who had leaned against Jesus at the last supper (see John 13:25 and 21:20). He was the disciple whom Jesus loved and to whom He entrusted His mother (see John 19:26-27). But John had also seen Jesus transfigured on the mountain. Now again, John sees Him in all His glory, and his heart is full of awe and wonder. Jesus is beyond being just a friend to John.

Intimacy with God is a treasure to be desired above all things, but greater intimacy with God does not lead to familiarity. In fact, almost the opposite is true. Because we can never fully grasp or understand Him, He will constantly amaze us. After more than three years of physically being with Jesus day and night, and many subsequent years walking with Jesus in the Spirit, John is more worshipful and reverent towards Him than ever. When Jesus speaks to John "the beloved," He speaks like a trumpet, and awakens John's spiritual senses, causing him to change position. The voice turns John around and calls him up.

Hearing God is a wonderful experience, but He doesn't necessarily get softer in tone the closer you get to Him! He can speak in "a gentle whisper" to a depressed prophet, like Elijah, who is expecting a voice more like a hurricane (see 1 Kings 19:12). But here, He talks to a man who is probably His closest friend on the earth—His most faithful and obedient pastor, who has suffered as much as any for the gospel—and He speaks like a trumpet to calls him onwards and upwards. Such a God is easier to worship; He demands respect. He knows when to comfort us with His love, and He knows when to speak to us like a King. When the King speaks, His voice moves us and stirs us out of lethargy and discouragement to call us up into all that He has for us.

The Invitation to Ascend

"Come up!" says the voice like a trumpet. This is a call that the Jewish listeners would understand. At Mount Sinai, a "very loud" trumpet blast from the mountain drew people towards God's presence. The trumpet sound got louder and louder as they got closer, until the voice called Moses to come up and meet with Him (see Exod. 19:16-20). There, on the mountain, God explained His plans to His servant, so that Moses, in turn, could tell God's people. The trumpet voice in Revelation calls John up through the door for the same purpose: *"Come up here and I will show you what must take place after this"* (Rev. 4:1).

The week before I was to speak on this passage, I had read the story of Jacob's ladder to my one-and-a-half-year-old daughter. The next morning, I had come downstairs to do my devotions and Jessica came down with me. As I was getting ready to pray, I could hear her saying, "Up, Daddy! Up!" again and again. Finally, I looked over at her, and she was looking at the picture of Jacob in our picture Bible. She was pointing to the ladder and saying, "Up, Daddy! Up!"

That was one of those spine-tingling "God moments," and I got the message. I believe that the invitation is there for us all. In the Hebrew mind, ascendancy was always linked to worship—whether it was Mount Moriah, Mount Sinai, or Mount Zion. A call to worship would include the encouragement of "Let's go up." Perhaps we need to revisit this glorious truth if we are to grow in our worship. The question is: "How are we supposed to 'go up'?"

The Truth About Ascendancy

The truth is that our ascendancy is not based on anything we can do; our ascendancy is in Christ alone. Ephesians 1:15–2:10 clearly outlines the journey of our "going up" into heavenly places. The passage starts with a prayer that we may understand more of who God is (see Eph. 1:17) and all that He has done for us (see Eph. 1:18). In answer to his own prayer, Paul, by the Holy Spirit, explains how God the Father took Jesus from death itself and raised Him into the heavenly realms by *"the working of His mighty strength"* (Eph. 1:19). Then, Paul explains that we too were in tombs of our own;

"dead" in our transgressions and sins (see Eph. 2:1). What hope is there for ascendancy if we are dead?

But, in Christ, the dead are raised, and it's not just at the final trumpet on the last day. In Christ, we are not merely resurrected from the dead, as wonderful and exciting as that is. The resurrection was not the end of Jesus' journey, and it is not the end of the journey for us. Christ ascended to the highest place in Heaven and earth (see Phil. 2:12), seated at the right hand of the Father in the heavenly realms (see Eph. 1:3). In Him, we also ascend to where He is seated in the highest place. If we are in Christ, this is not a future hope for when Jesus comes again; this has already been done and it is a present reality. Here is how Paul explains the journey that we have already taken:

> But because of His great love for us, God, who is rich in mercy, made us alive with Christ even when we were dead in transgressions—it is by grace you have been saved. And God raised us up with Christ and seated us with Him in the heavenly realms in Christ Jesus, in order that in the coming ages He might show the incomparable riches of His grace, expressed in His kindness to us in Christ Jesus (Ephesians 2:4-7).

If our ascendancy is in Christ and happens to us at the moment of our conversion, how is it that John has to be invited back up? Surely, in Christ, he is already there. From a positional standpoint, we are in Christ—seated with Him in heavenly realms—but the fullness of that reality will not come to us until Jesus returns. Then, we will see Him *"face-to-face"* (see 1 Cor. 13:12). However, what happens here to John is that he is suddenly, albeit temporarily, ushered into the fullness of what God has in store for all of us.

One could argue that this was a special, unique experience for a special and unique person, and that we should not expect it to happen to us before we are taken to be with God. However, it is difficult to get away from the context of John's journey into Heaven. Jesus has just encouraged members of the Laodicean church to buy eye salve so that they could see. Why did they need the eye salve? Obviously, they needed it to see clearly and come into reality about their own spiritual state. But, more important-ly, they needed eye salve to give them a fresh vision of the God whom they professed to worship.

The truth is that we may not all get "caught up into the third heaven" in the way that John did. Paul seemed to indicate that such an experience was unusual for Christians (see 2 Cor. 12:1-6). However, we can ask for eye salve to see more; we can ask for greater revelation to know Him better. The God who encourages us to ask, obviously wants to answer our prayers. So, when we ask, we should do so in faith and trust that God will not disappoint but will bless us by giving sweet, precious glimpses of the reality awaiting us in Heaven. Although, from a positional standpoint, John is already ascended in Christ and seated with Him in the heavenly realms, "the beloved" is still earthbound physically. Yet, here, he finds him-self in the reality of all that he longs for.

Ascending in the Spirit

Our ascendancy is given to us in Christ. But what transported John into this unique and wonderful experience of all that Jesus died to give us? The answer is in the text's next phrase (see Rev. 4:2). Having received the invitation to come up, John was "at once...in the spirit" and transported into Heaven itself. The call of Jesus always comes with His divine and supernatural enabling, and this little phrase offers another important key to finding our way into a deep-er place of worship. The call is to "come up" to somewhere that no man or woman can reach in their physical state. In order to enter Heaven and worship, we need to be alive "in spirit."

John already understood this principle from the discourse between Jesus and the woman at the well. Jesus said to her, *"God is spirit, and His worshipers must worship in spirit and in truth"* (John 4:24). Note the imperative in this statement: Anyone who wishes to worship *must* worship in spirit. The Greek phrase here is exact-ly the same as that used by John to describe his state in Revelation 4:2, as opposed to what John uses in Revelation 1:10, 17:3, and 21:10;

the latter three verses refer to being in "the Spirit," which is the third person of the Trinity. By contrast, the phrase in Revelation 4:2 and John 4:24 seems not to refer to the Holy Spirit's person, so much as a conscious state of mind and being: "in spirit." It is not an easy concept to understand or explain and may be best understood in the sense of "not being in the flesh." Somehow, we need to put aside the fleshly patterns of our natural minds and tune into the airwaves of Heaven.

Of course, what happened to John was involuntary; God did it to him. Rather than John reaching out to God, he received from God a gift of grace. In Luke 1, we already saw that God can supernaturally gift us with such an experience any time He chooses to—whether we are seeking Him in the right way or not (see this book's Introduction). The question then becomes, "Do we have any control of whether we are 'in the spirit' or not?" This is quite a huge question. If we have no control in this area, then we can only hope and pray for ascendancy in God, rather than be able to move towards it at any time.

Surely, being "in the spirit" begins with the indwelling of the Holy Spirit that makes us spiritually alive. Without this transformation, we cannot worship. This is perhaps why Jesus' discourse with Nicodemus about being born "of the Spirit" (see John 3) comes before His talk about true worship with the Samaritan woman (see John 4). Not only do we need the Holy Spirit to begin truly worshiping, but we need to "be filled with the Holy Spirit" (see Eph. 5:18) in order to continue worshiping. Notice that *"be filled with the Holy Spirit"* precedes *"sing and make music in your hearts to the Lord"* (Eph. 5:19). The Holy Spirit always moves us towards worship.

How Do We Go on Being Filled With the Spirit?

The Holy Spirit is a gift we can ask for more of. Jesus said, *"...how much more will your heavenly Father in heaven give the Holy Spirit to those who ask Him"* (Luke 11:13). So praying in faith is part of the answer. But, biblically, there is more to growing in things of the Spirit than simply asking.

In Romans 8, Paul gives us a balanced view. "In Christ," we are free from condemnation (verse 1) and, therefore, free to approach God. However, we need to be freed from control of our sinful natures to go on pleasing God (verse 8). To be freed from control of our sinful nature, we need to live "according to the Spirit" (verse 4). To live according to the Spirit requires us to have our "minds set on what the Spirit desires" (verse 5), and to partner with the Holy Spirit in putting to death the "misdeeds of the body" (verse 13). This is an "obligation" for us.

So then, having received the gift of the Holy Spirit as an essential part of our salvation, we have an obligation to partner with the Spirit now alive in us. We do this by participating with the grace available to us in Jesus; this is done by setting our minds on what pleases Him and by putting to death the misdeeds of our flesh. The implication is that this is how a saved person grows as a spiritual being, rather than as a carnal one. Such a person is much more likely to be found "in the spirit," as opposed to someone who is not partnering with God's grace in this way.

Being "in the spirit" then is a skill that can be learned, and it's not just an experience you have to wait for. If we want to be "in the spirit," then we simply need to partner with the Holy Spirit in moving us away from being "in the flesh." If this is true, Heaven is a lot more accessible and true worship much more probable.

What Does This Mean Practically?

In practical terms, this might mean throwing off discouragement and anxiety before coming to worship. It may mean apologizing to your spouse and children for getting frustrated when they weren't ready on time. Perhaps, it means actively taking steps to deal with some sinful patterns in our lives. Whatever that reality may be for us, we must learn to become skilled at "putting off the flesh." We do that by setting our minds on heavenly things, if we want to be "in the spirit" while worshiping.

In that sense, true worship may be better judged by a few criteria: whether we are free of bitterness towards others; have no unconfessed sin in our hearts; and are living in obedience to God's call on our lives, rather than on what "feels good." If we are not moving from a life lived "in the flesh" towards one "in the spirit," then singing powerful songs of praise and dedication may not help us to worship.

Personally, I have become more cautious about some of my declarations in worship. I am finding that I cannot easily sing phrases like, "I am giving You all my life" or "I am fully Yours" or even "I will always worship You." I take a look inside my heart and realize that those words aren't totally true for me. I can more truthfully sing such noble sentiments as a desire that I have, as opposed to a reality I always live in. In that way, although I am not always "in the spirit," at least I am being honest in my worship. I believe that God will not refuse such an offering.

Maybe, this is partly what Jesus meant when He talked about worshiping *"in spirit and in truth"* (John 4:23). In the same verse, Jesus describes people who worship with this combination of spirit and truth as being "true worshipers." In reality, the link between "in spirit" and "in truth" is so close that you cannot really distinguish one from the other. Why is being "in the spirit" so necessary for worship? Simply put, you can't drag your flesh into Heaven with you. If you're going into Heaven to worship before His throne, then you have to leave the flesh behind. You can't "go up" unless you go up "in the spirit." When we learn to be "in the spirit," we will move into greater worship. In Revelation 4, John, while "in the spirit," finds Heaven opening up before him.

Where Do We Worship?

The need to "go up" was crucial for the early Church to understand. The whole discourse between Jesus and the woman at the well in John 4:19 centers around the place of our worship. To the Samaritan, worship was "on this mountain," but to the Jew it was "in Jerusalem," more specifically in the temple. Both required going up, but Jesus was thinking of another location for worship. By the time the first century came to a close, worshiping in the temple at Jerusalem was not an option. The Romans had destroyed the temple in a.d. 70. This rocked the faith of many Jewish Christians. Knowing whether the Book of Hebrews was written before or after its destruction would certainly have helped to answer a lot of questions that must have been on those early Christians' minds. There, in Hebrews, the place of our worship is redefined.

The Jews obviously used to worship in an earthly location—the tabernacle or the temple. When Christ came, He opened the way to the *"more perfect tabernacle that is not man-made, that is to say not a part of this creation"* (Heb. 9:11). Through His blood, He made a way to a place of worship higher than even the temple in Jerusalem. *"For Christ did not enter a man-made sanctuary that was only a copy of the true one; He entered heaven itself, now to appear for us in God's presence"* (Heb. 9:24). As a result, that is now where we worship as well.

"Therefore, brothers, since we have confidence to enter the Most Holy Place [not the most holy place on earth, but *the* Most Holy Place, even Heaven itself] *by the blood of Jesus...let us draw near to God"* (Heb. 10:19,22). For *"You have not come to a mountain that can be touched* [a physical location]...*But you **have come*** [this is not a future experience] *to Mount Zion, to the heavenly* [not the earthly] *Jerusalem, the city of the living God. You **have come** to thousands upon thousands of angels in joyful assembly, to the church of the firstborn...You **have come** to God"* (Heb. 12:18,22 emphasis added).

This is a sneak preview of Revelation 4 and 5: The place of our worship is not on the earth but is in Heaven! It is not a physical place, but it is a spiritual place. This is crucial to the argument of this book and why it is entitled *Heavenly Worship*. If our worship is merely on earth, then why do we need eye salve to see beyond the natural into Heaven itself? Why do we need to worship "in the spirit," if we can simply worship in an earthly location? This book is about heavenly worship because the place of our worship is in Heaven! We have to go up, if we are to worship. If there is no ascendancy, then we are worshiping in the wrong place.

The door to this place of worship is standing open. Heaven is accessible! The invitation has been given: "Come up." God wants us to ascend in Christ and—with empowering of the Holy Spirit—to move us where we could never be in our natural strength or gifting. Suddenly, Heaven is open to us, and we are welcomed into a worship service that, for once, we don't have to plan or initiate. Heavenly worship has been going on since before time began. As we gaze into the wonder set before us, our own worship takes on an eternal meaning that it never had before. "Come up," says the voice, "and I will show you what must take place after this."

CHAPTER 3

The Journey of Heavenly Worship

The Glorious Throne, the Precious Stones, the Perfect Storm, and the Blazing Fire

The door is open, so we ascend "in the spirit" at the invitation of the Word of God and suddenly we are in Heaven. With John, we are invited on a journey to the center of heavenly worship. What first confronts John is a person, the likes of whom he has never met before. Even seeing Jesus on the Mount of Transfiguration would not have prepared him for what he is seeing now. John recognizes that he doesn't have the vocabulary to begin to describe the One who is before him, so he confines his description to a simple comparison: *"The One who sat there had the appearance of jasper and carnelian"* (Rev. 4:3).

He can, however, more adequately paint a picture of what surrounds the Person who sits in such splendor. This does not mean that the furniture and attendants described in these verses are as important as Him who sits on the throne; it simply means that they are more easily described. John does not give a more full description of the throne, the creatures, and the elders because they were the focus of his attention; he does so because, in different ways, they help us to understand the One who has John's complete attention. They help him to describe what cannot be described.

No earthly language—no matter how poetic—has words to adequately describe the One John sees; He is utterly beyond description. Neither is there any earthly experience—no matter how awesome and majestic—that comes close to the One whom John is experiencing here. He is utterly beyond our imagination. So John describes what can be described and trusts that his readers will not get caught up by those elements that can be related to (such as thrones, rainbows, and storms), but rather will see them for what they are. These elements are meant to reflect the glory of Him who sits upon the throne, and to do so in terms that can be grasped by our finite imaginations and limited vocabularies.

The journey of heavenly worship does not lead us along a well-decorated pathway—past ornate furniture, wonderful architecture, awesome creatures, and finely adorned people—towards God. The journey of heavenly worship begins with God, proceeds through God, and ends with God as its ultimate destination. What appears along the way is meant to help us see more of His manifold glory. With that in mind, we must look at John's description of Heaven's landscape with the clear purpose of uncovering greater revelations about the God we worship.

The Glorious Throne

At once I was in the Spirit, and there before me was a throne in heaven with someone sitting on it (Revelation 4:2).

So, John finds himself confronted by a throne "with Someone sitting on it" and, as we shall see, it is quite a confrontation. The throne totally dominates the landscape. John does not immediately see angels, the 24 other thrones, the four living creatures, or how Heaven is furnished and decorated; he sees only a throne.

To get to see an earthly throne, you have to go through checkpoints, past guards, through outer rooms, and into an inner sanctuary; the throne probably sits at the end of a long room amidst some stunning décor. Once you get through the door of Heaven, however, the throne is the first object you meet—it doesn't need guards or remote cameras for protection because it's totally secure in itself. In fact, the throne is the checkpoint by which all must enter.

I live in the province of Manitoba in the prairies of Canada. These prairies are famous for their "big skies." On one occasion, I watched as a storm rolled in from the west. Two huge pillars of black clouds—one on the right and one on the left, and joined together by a lower cloud in the middle—created the impression of an enormous chair. The storm totally dominated the skyline. This vista gave me some perspective of what John was seeing. The throne in Heaven totally filled John's gaze.

Much could be said in an attempt to describe this throne. But rather than try to explain what it is—which is close to impossible—perhaps it is simpler to explain what it is not.

The Throne Is Not an Armchair

This is not the favorite, cozy old chair where relaxed, affable, amiable Dad sits with a remote control in front of the television of His creation. He is not flipping from scene to scene throughout history to keep up with what is going on, all while He waits for His kids to come home. The God of the Bible is not that sort of God; although the way we relate to Him can be dangerously close to this sort of wrong thinking.

He is constantly alert; He neither slumbers nor sleeps (see Ps. 121:3-4). He is not careless of what is happening in His creation. He may appear removed in the eyes of the world, but His presence and His power are imminent and immediate (see Acts 17:28b). You cannot approach Him carelessly (see Heb. 12:28-29), or shuffle in with a sloppy attitude (see Matt. 22:11-13). His presence demands awe and respect. In Psalm 99:5, the psalmist exhorts us, *"Exalt the Lord our God* [acknowledge how far above us He is] *and worship at His footstool; He is Holy."*

The Throne Is Not a Love Seat

There is no space on this throne for someone else to cozy up alongside God. The last few years have seen a refreshing, life-changing emphasis on the Fatherhood of God. If there is any danger in what has been taught, it is the tendency to become over-familiar and use terminology unhelpful to our understanding of how to approach Him. He is undoubtedly a Father who loves His children with a passion that we understand to only a small degree. He expresses His love to us in very real and practical ways.

However, this truth has to be balanced with the fact that—in all the views of Heaven in Scripture, whether through eyes of Old Testament patriarchs and prophets or New Testament disciples—the God we are introduced to is not one whom we can run up to and throw ourselves upon. We do not find people climbing up and sitting on God the Father's knee! Yet, it must be true that those sitting around the throne (the 24 elders of Revelation 4:4) feel tremendously loved and accepted as His children.

We can sometimes think that the greatest manifestations of love are physical, but that is not true. Love is most perfectly felt and experienced in the spiritual. The greatest love is not expressed body-to-body, but spirit-to-spirit. These elders and angels might not appear to be physically in God's embrace, but they are there spiritually. Here, they are more satisfied and fulfilled in His love than we will ever be on the earth. They do not feel lack because they are not on their Father's knee.

They are fully and completely loved, but they do not sing of love either here or anywhere in the Book of Revelation. They sing of worthiness and holiness. They are with God and in God, and yet there is distance here. He is "Holy! Holy! Holy!" That means He is set apart, and not just by a short gap. Biblically, the priests are "holy," the temple implements are "holy," and the saints are a "holy people." But God is "Holy! Holy! Holy!" Isaiah says of Him, *I saw the Lord seated on a throne, high and exalted"* (Isa. 6:1). He is above us and beyond us and yet, somehow, remains totally accessible.

The Throne Is Unassailable

The security of the throne does not rely on walls, ramparts, and heavily armed guards; it is secure, not because of concrete foundations, but because of the constant character of He who sits on it. Psalm 97:2 declares, *"righteousness and justice are the foundation of His throne."* Here is absolute purity and holiness. In all of history and eternity, God has never had one wrong thought, bad attitude, or selfish motivation. He has never made a bad decision, a mistake, or any wrong turns. No one needs to defend Him, and He doesn't need to defend Himself—it is impossible to find fault with Him!

The Throne Is Not Under Threat From Within

Nineteenth century writer H.G. Wells once wrote of a Mr. Polly, who was a man with so many inner conflicts that he was "not so much a person, more a civil war." There is no civil war in God. He has a variety of seemingly opposing attributes. He loves the world, yet He requires righteous judgment. He is tender and kind, but can also be angry. His presence can inspire awful fear or unspeakable joy. This is not divine schizophrenia! All these characteristics of God and His glories are held together in tension, yet without tension! The One who sits upon the throne is totally at peace within Himself, who He is, and how He operates.

The Throne Is Not Self-Serving or Exclusive

Again, the opposite is true: This throne is embracing. Twenty-four elders, who represent the saved sinners of the two covenants, are seated royally in the circle of His authority (see Rev. 4:4). Their joy is His joy! He delights in including them and sharing who He is with them. This desire to share Himself is seen from the beginning of time when the three persons of the Godhead decide together, *"Let Us make man in Our image, in Our likeness"* (Gen. 1:26). It is powerfully underscored on Calvary where the same Godhead was amazingly "pleased" (see Isa. 53:10) to crush the glorious Son so that we could have a part in His glory. No, there is nothing selfish about this throne; it is the most generous, benevolent, self-sacrificing, and embracing place in all the universe.

The Throne Is Not Symbolic

Many of the world's thrones have largely become relics of a past authority. Nowadays, if a throne is still used, it often has no real power—it is symbolic. That could not be said of this throne! Here is the seat of total, supreme, all-powerful, and unassailable authority. No part of creation or Heaven is outside of its rule and reign, and it cannot be overthrown, rivaled, or argued against. This throne cannot be put to one side as irrelevant, nor can it be used to rubber stamp mankind's decisions. On the contrary, this throne is the center of the universe and, "in the spirit," it fills our field of vision, captures our imagination, and captivates our hearts. It becomes the center of our worship and of our very lives!

The Throne Is Not Empty

"And there before me was a throne in heaven with someone sitting on it" (Rev. 4:2). What a powerful truth this is. The seat of supreme power is occupied by Someone who cannot be described in terms that we humans know and understand. The throne has always been occupied by the same Person, and it will *always* be occupied by the same Person: *"from everlasting to everlasting You are God!"* (Ps. 90:2). He is not going to retire or throw off His responsibilities to find a quieter life. He loves being God; He always has and He always will! At the beginning of this chapter, I said that John—in his journey to the center of worship—is first confronted by the throne. It is certainly a confrontation! The throne asks this question:"WILL YOU BOW TO HIM?"

The throne exposes issues of sovereignty, control, and authority in our lives. If we want to go further into Heaven, we have to settle these issues, and probably not do so just once, but again and again. We have to bend to His supreme and total lordship of our lives. However, this need not be the bowing of a defeated foe. We have the option of being captivated by His love, even before we are inevitably captive to His power. He has set Himself to win our hearts rather than trample on our necks. The choice is ours to make while we still have the breath of this life in us. We need to realize that this bowing is not the end of heavenly worship, but just the beginning. We "come up" to bow down!

The Precious Stones

1. Jasper and Carnelian

"And the one who sat there had the appearance of jasper and carnelian" (Rev. 4:3). If that is a description of the throne, what about the One who sits on it? John can only describe Him in terms of precious stones, such as "jasper and carnelian." Here, there is more than just awesome power and tender mercy; there is incredible beauty! God has filled the earth with beautiful things, whether small and delicate like a flower or a hummingbird, or large and expansive like a prairie sunset. His creation is a reflection of who He is. When we create, the possibility exists that we can create something a lot more awe-inspiring than ourselves. That possibility does not exist for God!

On the morning of January 16, 2002, I sat at home looking out of our family room and wrote this to the Lord in my journal: "It's beautiful outside today—snow-covered trees, a blanket of white, and the sun hasn't even come up yet. Thank You for beauty." The reply that came to me was, "There is much more beauty to be seen in Heaven than anything that can be found on earth." The most beauty that can be seen—either in Heaven or on earth—is to be found in Him who sits upon the throne, and that beauty is one worth gazing upon!

One thing I ask of the Lord, this is what I seek: that I may dwell in the house of the Lord all the days of my life, to gaze upon the beauty of the Lord and to seek Him in His temple (Psalm 27:4).

The appearance of Him who sits on the throne asks a second question: Will you cherish Him?

Our eldest daughter, Lucy, developed a treasure trove of "precious things" at a young age. They were not valuable because they were worth a lot of money; rather, their value had to do with the meaning that they held for her. If a special friend gave an item to her, then it became precious—even if it was a scrap of paper with some illegible scribbles on it. Another "precious thing" (as we came to call them) was a small, transparent bouncy-ball with a dolphin in the middle. This was precious because it was the first item Lucy ever bought with her own money.

After giving her a small amount of money to spend while on holiday, we took her to a shop where she could spend it. Having shown her everything she could buy, Lucy wanted the ball and wouldn't be persuaded otherwise; a year later, she still carried the ball in her purse. Lucy would take great care of these items and could always tell you where they were, even if she hadn't played with them for a while.

If one such item was lost or broken, her distress would amount to a period of grieving. Dismissing such tears as over-dramatic (as I'm sure sometimes they were) would be easy. However, it was impossible to deny how deeply attached Lucy was to her "precious things." The items in themselves didn't hold that much importance, but what they represented is what so affected her.

Thinking back on those times when her little heart would break, I can see something of how God has made us. Our heart is like a treasure box. We store up (for good or evil) what we choose to cherish. However, the heart is not made to be a strong safe; what it carries can be easily stolen, and we can be easily hurt. I worried that if Lucy consistently lost treasures, then she would harden her heart to protect herself from further pain. Suddenly, she might start to pretend, and then believe, that precious things don't matter so much any more. If Lucy started to devalue the gifts, then she would also begin to devalue the giver.

The fact is that precious things do matter. If we harden our heart to the need to value and cherish precious things, then we begin to lose some of our ability to cherish the God who gave us *"every good and perfect gift"* (James 1:17). Within each human is a cry for something of real beauty and ultimate value that the heart can be set upon without fear of disappointment. God has given us many gifts to enjoy and treasure, but ultimate value and worth is to be found in the Father who gave them to us.

When we say that a God-shaped vacuum exists in every heart, it means that at our core is a treasure box deliberately designed to fit only one "precious thing": the Person who sparkles like jasper and carnelian upon the throne of Heaven. Of course, God is too huge to fit into a small box. So, we discover that the God-shaped vacuum inside us is not a four-inch cube, but a hole about the size of the Grand Canyon. Great is the grief and loneliness of anyone whose treasure chest is empty!

This tells us something else about heavenly worship: Not only does there need to be a bowing ("You are Lord"), but also a cherishing ("You are worthy"). These are not simply the words to a song—they are a heartfelt expression of how precious God is to us. We are saying that He is of great worth and value. Worship should include time to reflect and meditate; we are to set this sparkling treasure before our eyes and give ourselves time to be awed and amazed. We must take time to allow our hearts to once again feel how precious He is to us. If our hearts are soft, then, like Lucy, any sense of distance between us and our most prized possession should be a matter of feeling real pain.

> *All night long on my bed I looked for the one my heart loves; I looked for him but did not find him. I will get up now and go about the city, through its streets and squares; I will search for the one my heart loves. So I looked for him but did not find him. The watchmen found me as they made their rounds in the city. "Have you seen the one my heart loves?" Scarcely had I passed them when I found the one my heart loves. I held him and would not let him go...* (Song of Solomon 3:1-4a).

This could have been Mary Magdalene's song during the night of the Cross and the morning of the resurrection. Her treasure was missing, and she was distraught. Then she found Him, or, rather, He found her, and she would not let Him go (see John 20:10-17).

It is amazing that God would take the "precious things" of Heaven and put them inside our own poor hearts, but He does. *"We have this treasure* [of the glory of God] *in jars of clay"* (2 Cor. 4:7), and it is a treasure worth cherishing and guarding. *"Will you cherish Him?"* is really asking the question: "WILL YOU GIVE HIM THE PREEMINENT PLACE IN YOUR HEART AS YOUR GREATEST TREASURE?"

God Sparkles

In his book *Reversed Thunder: The Revelation of St. John and the Praying Imagination*, author Eugene Peterson points out that, "Precious stones are precious because they collect and intensify light." The One who sits upon the throne, however, is not collecting light from outside of Himself; that light is coming from within Him. In fact, He is the source of all light! *"God is light,"* says *"the beloved"* in his first letter (see 1 John 1:5), *"in Him is no darkness at all."* John knew what he was talking about. He had been with Jesus on the Mount of Transfiguration when Jesus was revealed for who He really was and *"His clothes became as bright as a flash of lightning"* (Luke 9:29).

This eternal and internal light makes God sparkle like jasper and carnelian in every part of who He is and in everything He does. His justice sparkles—it is so clean, pure, true, and so free of any hypocrisy or selfishness. His creativity sparkles, with such an incredible imagination—it's enough beauty and diversity to fill a universe with unending wonders and mysteries. Some of these we will never find out about before Jesus returns; they are there simply because God enjoys the process of creating. All His glories make Him sparkle in various unique ways. Amazingly, part of the purpose of having this treasure in our hearts is so that we can sparkle for His glory.

2. THE EMERALD

A rainbow, resembling an emerald, encircled the throne (Revelation 4:3b).

The first two precious stones mentioned here—jasper and carnelian—encourage us to cherish and be awed by the beauty of Him who sits upon the throne. The next precious stone—the emerald—

tells us what to cherish above all about this God we worship. Around all the attributes of God's character sits a rainbow that is "resembling an emerald." But something else glitters and sparkles around the throne that encompasses and defines it.

Ezekiel describes the same sight as follows: *"Like the appearance of a rainbow in the cloud on a rainy day, so was the radiance around Him"* (Ezek. 1:28). There is some debate about whether this means a literal rainbow, or a halo of light shaped like a rainbow. The fact that the word *"rainbow"* is used to describe the same sight—both in Revelation and Ezekiel—seems to point towards it at least having the appearance of a literal rainbow.

That possibility opens a number of wonderful doors for interpretation. A rainbow in the Bible has great significance—it is a sign to us of God's covenant mercy. In the natural, a rainbow occurs at the meeting place between rain and sunshine. For Noah and his family, the rainbow came at the meeting place between God's judgment (the rain) and His mercy (the warm and drying sunshine). The sign of God's covenant mercy towards Noah was not just a rainbow, but a rainbow *"set...in the clouds"* (Gen. 9:13). In other words, it was mercy set in the backdrop of judgment.

This awesome and fearful throne in Heaven is intimidating and appears like a full-blown storm (see Rev. 4:5). However, in this place we only see lightning and hear thunder after we have seen the rainbow. God's perfect storm is wrapped around by the overriding glory of His covenant mercy. The rainbow of His mercy is the gold band into which is set the diamond of every other part of His character. When God showed His glory to Moses, He said: *"The Lord, the Lord God, merciful and gracious, longsuffering and abounding in goodness and truth, keeping mercy for thousands, forgiving iniquity and transgression and sin..."* (Exod. 34:6-7 NKJ).

In all probability, the rainbow in Heaven existed before God revealed one to Noah. Does that take the meaning of Noah's sign to a different level for us? Could it mean that God's own glory has

come down to begin surrounding the earth just as it already surrounds the throne? To God, this was not just another rainbow that
He put in the sky; in His own words, it was "*My* rainbow" (Gen.
9:13). Perhaps He was saying, "This rainbow that surrounds Me in
Heaven, representing My covenant mercy. I am going to set this
rainbow, My rainbow, over the earth too."

Whether that is a true interpretation or not, the awesome and
fearful throne set before us in Revelation 4 is made more welcome
to a nervous saint by the rainbow surrounding it! The One who
sits upon the throne has all power and authority. We stand before
Him deserving judgment, but He has wrapped all His character
with mercy, and we can find forgiveness and acceptance here.

3. THE CRYSTAL

*Also before the throne there was what looked like a sea of glass, clear
as crystal* (Revelation 4:6).

Crystal is not a precious stone, but it represents another attrib-
ute of God's character. That "sparkle" is one we would do well to
cherish. The obvious message of this crystal sea is God's absolute,
transparent purity and holiness. No blemish, spot, or shadow can
be found in Him. God's eternity is of absolute purity in every
action, every word, every thought, and every motivation of His
heart. His holiness sparkles, especially set against the backdrop of
our own sinfulness. For us to not be able to understand God's
heart would be a disheartening and discouraging sight and cause
permanent distance and division between us and the Lord whom
we wish to imitate and worship.

This "sea" is also recorded in Ezekiel's vision of the throne:
"*Spread out above the heads of the living creatures was what looked like an
expanse, sparkling like ice, and awesome*" (Ezek. 1:22). In Ezekiel's
vision, the sea is underneath the throne and separates God from
the earth; the sea separates us from Him because, outside of
Christ, we are so transparently sinful by comparison.

However in Revelation 4, the saints, now in Christ, are also gathered around that purity; no longer is it a dividing line, but the standard around which we all gather. He has not compromised His purity one iota. He is still crystal clear. We have been brought near to Him through the purifying work of the blood of Jesus. We have been brought up to His standard. In Christ, we are with Him, above the sea of His purity and in complete holiness.

Like His mercy and all His other glories, the purity of God sparkles. When we worship, we need to cherish His holiness in our hearts and, as we do so, we may sparkle more in this area as well. "Worthy, worthy" is the cry of a heart that has set apart this God whom we worship as the most prized and treasured of possessions. Such a cherishing is part of our journey into heavenly worship.

The Perfect Storm

From the throne came flashes of lightning, rumblings and peals of thunder (Revelation 4:5a).

This sight was another one familiar to the Jewish community. They first witnessed it when reaching Mount Sinai after having left Egypt. *"On the morning of the third day there was thunder and lightning, with a thick cloud over the mountain"* (Exod. 19:16). God brought the Israelites out of Egypt with the clear purpose of taking His people on a journey into worship. On numerous occasions, Moses stated this clearly to Pharaoh, with the message, *"The Lord, the God of the Hebrews, has sent me to say to you: Let My people go, so that they may worship Me in the desert"* (Exod. 7:16).

As we have recognized, worship needs to be fueled by revelation. In order to teach them how to worship, God took the Israelites on a journey through the wilderness. The desert's trials were deliberately designed to reveal God's different characteristics to the Hebrews, so that they could then worship. At first, the strategy appeared to work. In delivering His people from Pharaoh and the Egyptian army—by miraculously bringing them through the Red Sea on dry land—God revealed Himself as a warrior and savior. The Hebrews responded to God by worshiping Him for these attributes: *"The Lord is my strength and my song; He has become my salvation. He is my God, and I will praise Him, my father's God and I will exalt Him. The Lord is a warrior; the Lord is His name"* (Exod. 15:2-3).

God continued to lead them on a journey into worship. He revealed Himself as *"The Lord, who heals you"* (Exod. 15:26) at the Waters of Marah. By giving the Hebrews manna and quail in Exodus 16:1-36, He revealed Himself as the provider. As He brought water out of the rock at Rephidim (see Exod. 17:1-7), God revealed Himself as a present help, or the Lord who is there for His people. In Exodus 17:8-16, in fighting for His people against the Amalekites, He revealed Himself as *"the Lord our banner."* And in Exodus 18, He showed Himself to be a wonderful administrator who cares for His people's individual needs.

All of these revelations came out of crisis situations, and God fully met the need in each case. At first, such generosity produced worship, but then the people just became more and more miserable. God's kindness seemed to produce more whining than worship. They had seen God's hand, but not His face. They had become "fair-weather worshipers"; they were fine with God and Moses as long as everything was provided for them.

Thankfully, God did not give up on them. He brought them to Himself to teach them more about how to worship Him. When God came down on Sinai, He broke into their fair-weather lives with a terrifying storm. They were shaken by the awesome power revealed to them: *"Everyone in the camp trembled"* (Exod. 19:16). As the fear of God entered their hearts that day, they were shown another key ingredient on their journey into worship.

John is given the same revelation (see Rev. 4:5). God has not changed. He is as fearful as He ever was. Those who would worship Him should do so "acceptably with reverence and awe" (Heb. 12:28). We would be mistaken in thinking that the God of our eternity will somehow cease to be fearful. David is very clear that *"the fear of the*

Lord is pure, enduring forever" (Ps. 19:9). This is not the negative, destructive, and crippling fear that the devil seeks to sow into our lives. The fear of the Lord is healthy and life-giving. By embracing it, rather than running away, a quality of worship comes out of us that could not be experienced otherwise.

The Flashes of Lightning

Amidst this fearful storm, bolts of light come hurtling out like "flashes of lightning." From elsewhere in Scripture, we know that light emanating from Him who sits upon the throne is blindingly bright. The apostle Paul would attest to that, for it knocked him down and *"the brilliance of the light"* blinded him (see Acts 22:6,11). Peter, James, and John would also bear witness to this truth: As they saw Jesus transfigured before them, His very clothes became *"as bright as a flash of lightning"* (Luke 9:29). Heaven has no need for any other light source: *"They will not need...the light of the sun, for the Lord God will give them light..."* (Rev. 22:5).

Bolts of lightning are a fearful sight, especially when they appear to be directed straight at us, as in Paul's case. However, if we are to journey further in worship, we cannot run from them. As with Paul, these can be flashes of revelation. They reveal to us something of His glory, while at the same time revealing our own unworthiness and sin. They are sent to us to reveal, to heal, and to provoke greater and purer worship, *not* to kill and destroy. They may come to us as a bolt out of the blue while we listen to a sermon or sing a worship song. Or, they may come to us when we are simply going about the normal tasks of our daily lives. But when a bolt of lightning from the throne hits, you suddenly awaken into a whole new reality about God and yourself.

God lives in light, and He invites us to live there too (see 1 John 1:5-7). This means letting Him into the darkest part of our lives and inviting His correction and healing. What initially impacts us as wounding and even life-threatening, in the end can bring us into newness of life—if we embrace it. Inevitably, all who haven't called on the Lord's name will have to stand before the brilliance of His light. It is better to face the lightning now than in eternity, especially if we have a clear revelation of the kindness and love of the God from whom it emanates.

Here are three simple ways to walk in the light, as part of our journey in worship:

A. Let the Word In

"Your word is a lamp to my feet and a light for my path" (Ps. 119:105) and *"it judges the thoughts and attitudes of the heart"* (Heb. 4:12). We must read the Bible and listen to it being preached in an attitude of allowing ourselves to be judged. Sometimes, when we criticize the Word or the preacher the most, we are looking for an excuse to not face up to what God is saying to us.

B. Let the Spirit In

The Spirit is given to us as a guide and counselor. One way that He helps us is to convict us of areas of darkness in our lives (see John 16:8). Inviting Him to expose sinful patterns can seem threatening, but in reality we are more threatened by leaving those patterns hidden. We can always be assured that the Holy Spirit will deal with us in love.

C. Let Others In

Walking in the light means living in fellowship with God and others (see 1 John 1:7). James encourages us to *"confess your sins to each other and pray for each other so that you may be healed"* (James 5:16). If asking the Holy Spirit to expose sin is threatening, then it can be even more threatening to expose your own sin to brothers and sisters who have the grace to help you. However, it often ends up being a doorway into deeper fellowship—not only with God, but also with each other.

The perfect storm asks us a third question: "Will you fear Him?"

We are not living in the fear of the Lord, if we are running from Him. The correct response to the perfect storm and its bolts of lightning is not to hide, but to bow in His awesome presence and allow Him to do with us whatever He pleases.

❧

The glorious throne asks: WILL YOU BOW TO HIM?
The precious stones ask: WILL YOU CHERISH HIM?
The perfect storm asks: WILL YOU FEAR HIM?

❧

There is, however, one more question we are asked in our journey to the center of heavenly worship. This question may prove to be the most costly of all for us to respond to.

The Blazing Fire

Before the throne, seven lamps were blazing. These are the seven spirits of God (Revelation 4:5).

It is not left to our imagination to decide what the blazing torches represent because the writer tells us: Here, before the throne, is the burning fire of the Holy Spirit. Matthew 3:11 shows a clear contrast between the ministries of John the Baptist and that of Jesus. John baptizes in water, but Jesus baptizes in the Holy Spirit and in fire. John's water comes from the Jordan River; Jesus' fire comes from the seven blazing torches before the throne of God. The word for baptize in the Greek (*baptizo*) literally means to overwhelm. Jesus didn't come to give us a little touch of fire; He has come to overwhelm us with the Holy Spirit and fire.

On Mount Carmel, Elijah rebuilds the altar and overwhelms it with water (see 1 Kings 18:33-24). In fact, he does so three times. Physically, he did his part—just as John could physically baptize people in the Jordan River—but what happened next could only have come from the throne of God. *"Then the fire of the Lord fell and burned up the sacrifice, the wood, the stones and the soil, and also licked up the water in the trench"* (1 Kings 18:38). The fire completely overwhelmed and consumed the sacrifice. As we are confronted by the blazing torches before the throne in Revelation 4, we are asked a final question: "WILL YOU BURN FOR HIM?"

Consumerism is one of the major forces driving Western society. Unfortunately, that can quietly creep into our relationship with God. When we come into the presence of Almighty God, have we come to be consumers of the Holy Spirit, or have we come to be consumed by Him? Are we there for what He can *do* for us, or are we there for Him? In biblical times, there was no light without a burning flame. When Jesus said to His disciples, *"You are the light of the world"* (Matt. 5:14), He was not referring to an electric light bulb that can just be switched on. He was talking about a lamp or a candle, either of which needed to be ignited by fire. The more fiercely the flame burned, the more light it would give off. Jesus said that we are the light of the world. It's going to take a powerful flame to light up the whole earth!

Will we be consumed? As when we are faced with the storm, our first reaction might be to run away. But, if we did, we would lose out on the wonderful benefits that the fire offers. Each of these three questions is related to one another. The throne asks if we will bow, and we may gladly say "Yes." The precious stones ask us if we will give God the place of greatest treasure in our hearts, and, again, we may say "Yes."

Then, as the storm shakes us and the light pierces us, we are brought to a greater sense of reality about the true meaning of submission. We discover how deep some of our problems truly are. The problem can then be that we are left with an acute awareness of impotence against strongholds of sin and unbelief in our lives. As Christians, we have already received cleansing from the blood of Jesus, but we wrestle with ongoing issues of holiness and freedom in Christ.

So, then we come to the baptism of fire. John's water baptism was a ceremonial, outer cleansing. When Jesus comes, His baptism purges and refines us with the Holy Spirit's fire. That eternal flame is actually the answer to our longing for purity and power.

However, it is fire—it is hot and it burns! When James and John wanted to sit next to Jesus on His throne, Jesus asked them, *"Can you...be baptized with the baptism I am baptized with?"* (Mark 10:38). He was, of course, referring to the manner of His death.

We may not be literally crucified, but Jesus' baptism truly is one of fire and we will lose our lives in the process. We have one life to live on this earth. What are we going to burn for? What is going to arouse our greatest passions? What is going to move us the most and set the course of our destiny? Surely, there is no greater purpose than the glory of God. Surely, the Lamb is worthy of more than a half-hearted response. The Laodicean church was strongly rebuked for being "neither hot nor cold." The tepid nature of their hearts was reflected in "their deeds." Now, more than ever, it is time to burn with worship that pleases Heaven and lights up the world.

A few years ago, I stood on the spot in Oxford, England, where, in 1555, Hugh Latimer and Nicholas Ridley were burned at the stake for their faith. On arriving at the site of their execution, Latimer turned to his friend and said: "Be of good cheer, Master Ridley, and play the man, for we shall this day in England light such a candle that, by God's grace, shall never be put out." The fire of Heaven had consumed Latimer long before torches were put to the brushwood around his feet. The candle lit that day still burns 450 years later; God answered Latimer's dying prayer.

So, as we travel with John on his Spirit-led journey to the center of heavenly worship, we have to deal with issues of authority, worth, fear, and fire. The throne "without the stones" (or bowing without cherishing) can lead to cold, fearful, distant obedience, rather than one's selling everything for an unspeakable joy of holding the pearl of greatest price. The throne and the stones without the perfect storm (or bowing and cherishing without making ourselves vulnerable) can lead to unreality. We may believe we are submitting to His Lordship, but hidden areas of rebellion and pride lurk in our hearts.

The fear without the fire (or honesty without power) can lead to despair; we become trapped in discouragement at our lack of power over strongholds of sin in our spiritual walk. Having been hit by a heavenly bolt of lightning, Saul of Tarsus was left blind and helpless. God sent Ananias to Saul not just to heal his sight, but also to make sure that he was filled with the Holy Spirit's fire (see Acts 9:17).

Together, all the elements do an amazing work in the lives of broken humanity: They heal and restore us, but what they do for us is not most important. As we deal with what confronts us in Heaven, we truly do become lights for God and His glory upon the earth.

Together these heavenly elements give God a people of submission, softness, integrity, and power!

CHAPTER 4

The Center of Heavenly Worship

The Scroll, the Harp, and the Bowl

As John struggles to take in the sights surrounding him, he finds himself part of a glorious worship service. It begins with the four living creatures and moves through a wonderful progression to its climax at the end of Revelation 5. We will look more closely at that progression—and the creatures and people involved in it—in this book's last chapter. In the meantime, we set the scene by examining some of the landscape painted for us.

The Book of Revelation, chapter 4, has focused our attention on *"Him who sits upon the throne."* We have been invited to bow, to cherish, to be open and honest, and to burn. Only two objects of worship exist in Heaven: The first is "Him who sits upon the throne," and now Revelation 5 gloriously and dramatically unveils the second. However, we are not immediately introduced to Him. The journey to the center of worship must first take us past one more element.

The Scroll

Peering through the intense brightness that emanates from the throne, John begins to see an object through the glaring light. Held firmly in God's hand is a scroll, which was a normal part of Hebrew worship. In every synagogue meeting, someone would take up a scroll in hand. So, to the early Christians, seeing a scroll as part of a worship service in Heaven would be almost expected. This scroll, however, is a little different from those seen in earthly places of worship.

John notices writing on both sides, which was very unusual for papyrus scrolls of the time. However, any student of Hebrew history would immediately think of the stone tablets of the Testimony brought down the mountain by Moses. *"They were inscribed on both sides, front and back"* (Exod. 32:15). The fact that these stones were supernaturally inscribed on both sides underscores the authorship of the commandments; *"the tablets were the work of God; the writing was the writing of God, engraved on the tablets"* (Exod. 32:16). Here, in Revelation 5, Heaven possesses a scroll that supernaturally has writing on both sides. The obvious conclusion is that God Himself also wrote this scroll.

However, no one can read what is written because the scroll is sealed with seven seals. This scroll appears to represent hidden, impenetrable mysteries. The minds of the early Church possibly equated its seven seals with a person's last will and testament, which was often sealed in the same way. They may have interpreted what John saw as being the last will and testament of God concerning His purposes.

But before we can become too depressed at the thought of God's will being hidden from us, we are encouraged by a mighty angel's loud proclamation: "Who is worthy to break the seals and open the scroll?" God Himself wants the scroll opened—so much so, that the proclamation appears to have been heard in every part of Heaven and earth. The trouble is that *"no one in heaven or on earth or under the earth could open the scroll or even look inside it"* (Rev. 5:3).

Here, in the hand of God, is His last will and testament. It contains His plans for the summation of all things, including His strategies for defeating evil and triumphing in righteousness; also included are details of the inheritance to come to His children. To the early Church, the scroll represents information that would give them hope and encouragement to press on. Inside the scroll are all God's promises for their future.

However, every will needs an executor, someone with the power and authority to ensure that everything is carried out according to the wishes of the person wrote the will. The scroll in the hands of Him who sits upon the throne also requires an executor with the authority to open the seals. This is the only way that the will's heirs (in this case, the children of God) shall receive the full benefit of its contained promises. The call goes out to all Heaven and earth to find one worthy of the task, but no one is found. For an instant, it seems that the righteous will not receive their reward and that the devil and his minions will not meet justice. No wonder John broke down and wept and wept.

The Executor

"Then one of the elders said to me, 'Do not weep!'" (Rev. 5:5a). I need to hear this elder's voice so often! This is the voice of joyful hope at the point where I want to just break down, when I cannot see what I want to see and I cannot know what I want to know, when I have no answers for the questions of hurting people around me, and when darkness seems to be gaining the upper hand. *"Do not weep! See, the Lion of the tribe of Judah, the Root of David, has triumphed! He is able to open the scroll and its seven seals"* (Rev. 5:5).

The worthy one is identified by two of the Old Testament's strongest messianic titles. The promise of a lion from the tribe of Judah was as old as Jacob (see Gen. 49:8-12). Many Scriptures refer to the Messiah as coming from David's lineage, although, to be accurate, this does turn many of those prophecies on their heads. Often, He was referred to as a branch of David (see Jer. 33:15) or a shoot coming up from Jesse (see Isa. 11:1). Here, the truth is clearer: The Messiah did not come from them (although in the natural, He did)—they came from the Messiah. He is the Root of David. In

Revelation 22:16, He introduces Himself as both *"the Root and the Offspring of David."*

Either way, He is introduced to John in terms of great strength: He is a lion and the father of Goliath-slayers (the Root of David). This is the reason why He can open the scroll—He "has triumphed." He has already fought, conquered, and won a great victory. The importance of that becomes clearer in the Book of Revelation, chapter 6, when we learn what occurs when the scrolls are opened. War breaks out, and this cosmic battle ultimately decides the fate of the earth, the universe, and even Heaven itself. The enemy is strong, subtle, and bent on destruction. Whoever opens this scroll—thereby taking the will of God into His own hands—must be strong enough to deal with the consequences! He has to be a proven conqueror. The elder says that there is one!

So we look for the lion and the David who kills Goliaths, who is a mighty warrior to bring all God's plans to final completion and rout all the armies of evil. But what we see instead is...a lamb. The image is shocking because of its apparent vulnerability, but even more shocking is a lamb covered not with trophies of victory but scars of defeat, *"looking as if it had been slain"* (Rev. 5:6). His death was not a clean one; the Greek word used here is more aptly translated as "slaughtered." It's a vision of pitiful helplessness and powerlessness; the sheep is not even fully grown—one translation of the Greek word would be "lambkin." So, whoever, or whatever, this poor creature battled must have been particularly vicious and cruel.

I have seen a big male sheep be eaten alive by a dog that got the scent of blood. The ram stood frozen in fear, as hunks of its flesh were torn away. The sight was horrific. Here, in Heaven, is the One of whom Isaiah said: *"He was led like a lamb to the slaughter and as a sheep before her shearers is silent, so He did not open His mouth"* (Isa. 53:7). Here is John the Baptist's Lamb of God who takes away the sin of the world.

It is interesting that this is not primarily my lamb or our lamb, but it is God's Lamb! Abraham had promised his son Isaac that

"God Himself will provide the lamb" (Gen. 22:8) and so He did! A Hebrew sinner could bring a young, spotless lamb to the altar as a sacrifice for sins. This cannot have been a pleasant experience. Some of us find it difficult enough to consider an animal being killed for food, let alone slaughtering one as punishment for our own sin. Perhaps it would quietly go to the place of sacrifice, or maybe it would struggle and bleat as you carried it in your arms. Then, by placing your hands on the animal, the sins of humanity would be ceremonially transferred onto it before its killing. Sin is ugly and messy!

From the Book of Hebrews, we know that these sacrifices could not completely cleanse the consciences of sinners who had brought them (see Heb. 9:9), so God provided Himself a lamb that could. We didn't bring the lamb, God did. We didn't lay hands on the lamb and speak our sins onto it, but God laid His hands on His own Lamb and spoke the world's sin onto Him. *"We all, like sheep, have gone astray, each of us has turned to his own way and the Lord has laid on Him the iniquity of us all"* (Isa. 53:6).

"God presented Him as a sacrifice of atonement, through faith in His blood" (Rom. 3:25). What a crushing weight! He had to bear the world's sins, the cruel spite of the prince of darkness and his hordes of wickedness, and heaviest of all, the awful anger of God His Father. No wonder the Lamb looks so broken! But in this hour of great need—with the destiny of all at stake—why turn to Him again? How can God put all the weight on these bruised, beaten shoulders for His will to be worked out for the end of the age? With more eye salve, we see a little clearer. First of all, we discover—even though it's horribly scarred and "looking as if it had been slain"—that this Lamb is not lying down. He is standing! He is *"standing in the center of the throne"* (Rev. 5:6)! He is alive!!

Often in a sports game, a team surrounds a teammate who is lying in agony on the ground. The other players huddle around the wounded colleague in a show of support. The Lamb is not standing in the center of the throne for protection, or to give Him a chance to recover. You would be mistaken if you thought Him to be weak and helpless. Closer inspection reveals that He has seven horns, which indicate perfect and total power and authority. He has seven eyes, which means He is perfect in wisdom and knowledge. These seven eyes are the seven Spirits of God. He is full of all the fullness of God.

For God was pleased to have all His fullness dwell in Him (Colossians 1:19).

For in Christ all the fullness of the deity lives in bodily form... (Colossians 2:9).

In this Lamb, the seven Spirits of God are *"sent out into all the earth"* (Rev. 5:6). In Revelation 4:5, they were like blazing torches before the throne, but now, in Christ, the Spirit is poured out on all flesh. This Lamb is a lion! He is a Goliath-slayer! Every destructive weapon in Heaven and earth was unleashed upon Him, including the wrath of God. He endured it all while hanging on a cross with His hands tied, and did not do so in defiance, anger, or grim determination, but in meekness and humility. He took it all on Good Friday, and then His Father lifted Him out of the tomb early on Sunday morning. Then, He went straight back to work encouraging and teaching His disciples, before being transported into Heaven where He now stands. He did not stop to lick His wounds. Indeed, the thought wouldn't have occurred to Him.

He has triumphed! (See Revelation 5:5.) This is a great encouragement to Sardis, Philadelphia, and Laodicea, which are the churches mentioned in Revelation 3. Each review ends with wonderful promises, which is typical of how Jesus leads His Church. These promises, however, all come with the same condition: They are for "him who overcomes." That would have felt like a tough assignment, especially to those facing possible torture and death. But then they read Revelation 5 and realized that, despite everything, the Lamb has already conquered. If He has triumphed, then He can lead them to victory too! *"But thanks be to God, who always leads us in triumphal procession in Christ..."* (2 Cor. 2:14).

Now, here He is in Heaven. However tough His previous assignment had been, He is eager to go on pleasing His Father. *"My food,"* said Jesus, *"is to do the will of My Father who sent Me..."* (John 4:34). However, simply doing His will wasn't enough: He adds, *"...and to finish His work."* Now, that's the heart of a lion! So, *"He came..."* (Rev. 5:7). Whenever the will of God needs to be done, Jesus comes! He came, He comes, and He will come again! And, He always comes at just the right time!

"He came and took the scroll out of the right hand of Him who sat on the throne" (Rev. 5:7). What boldness! If you didn't understand, you would call it arrogance! But, the Lamb can take from the right hand of God—whereas the arrogant and proud cannot—because He is clothed in the Lamb's wool of humility. The Lamb takes the will of God into His own hand! He didn't have to be asked or cajoled! Not long after God's will has taken Him to the Cross, He's back again! He doesn't just "take" the will of God—more accurately He "lays hold" of it (*lambano* in the Greek). Why could He do this? Psalm 40:7 gives the answer: *"Here I am, I have come—it is written about Me in the scroll. I desire to do Your will, O My God, Your law is within My heart."* He could do it because the will of God is, primarily, His to do.

He could do God's will because the scroll is all about Him. As always, the scroll has led us to the Son of God! He is the key to unlocking the great mysteries of God. In fact, Paul, in writing to the Colossians, says that Jesus actually is *"the mystery of God...in whom are hidden all the treasures of wisdom and knowledge"* (Col. 2:2-3). And He could do it because the Father knew that He could completely trust His purposes into the hands of His Son.

Isaiah 53:10 says, *"...and the will of the Lord will prosper in His hand."* The will of God is prospering in the hands of the Lamb! This was true for the early Christian Church, and it was just what they needed to know amidst all their troubles and persecutions. Two thousand years later, this still remains true! God's will is prospering in the hands of Jesus Christ. So what is the Church's response?

The Harp

The Lamb has the scroll in His hand; He has laid hold of it. The 24 elders also have their hands full. In one hand, they have a harp (see Rev. 5:8). In Revelation 15:2, we discover that God gave harps to *"those who had been victorious...."*

My wife Julia and I once watched a moving documentary film based on the true story of a woman who adopted a severely mentally handicapped boy. This film—*The Woman Who Willed a Miracle*—is a powerful illustration of what is happening in Revelation 5. The boy was so handicapped that he could not stand up or move by himself, and he could not communicate or show any form of emotion. The mother, a devout woman, prayed for him and tried to encourage him to respond to her; one way she did so was by getting her husband to carry the boy to their fence so he could try to hold himself up and, in time, even move. Over a period of years, the boy made some slow progress, but he still did not communicate in any way.

The parents loved to listen to music on TV, and, one day, the mother noticed that the boy was moving his fingers to the music. So, she asked her husband to get him a piano. The mother tried to get him to sit at the piano and put his fingers on the keys, but again nothing seemed to register with the boy. But one night, while the woman lay in bed with her husband, she heard beautiful piano music playing. Thinking that the TV had been left on, she went downstairs to turn it off, only to discover that it wasn't the TV at all! The boy was sitting at the piano, perfectly playing melodies he had heard on the television. He was later confirmed to be an idiot savant, which means that even though he could not function in most capacities, he was abnormally gifted in one area.

Playing the piano soon opened up his abilities to communicate in other ways. A while later, the boy was playing and singing for a group of neighborhood children, when, suddenly, he began to cry. This was the first time he had ever cried! The mother asked him what he was feeling. All he could say was "love." When she asked him to explain further, he began to play a famous old hymn:

"Amazing grace, how sweet the sound

That saved a wretch like me.

I once was lost but now I'm found,

Was blind but now I see."

—John Newton (1779)

This story is very moving, but it bears the same point as what is happening in Heaven. Before the throne of God, as we come from sinful brokenness, we are totally incompetent in ourselves of producing anything that pleases Him. Most of us are so dulled in our emotions that we can't even cry! But, then, we get touched by the mercy and grace of God—as revealed to us in the Lamb—and, suddenly, our heartstrings are plucked in a way that produces a worship that we didn't believe ourselves to be capable of.

This is not the natural music of people trained to play instruments; this is supernatural worship. We were created to worship, but the beauty of what we could produce was spoiled and tarnished by our sin. In fact, we turned our skills toward worshiping other gods! But now, here is dulled creation coming truly alive. God gives us harps so that we can play beautiful music and fill Heaven and earth with knowledge of His glory.

This, again, is a great encouragement. Most of us truly have little idea of the potential that God has given us in this area. Like the *idiot savant*, we are trapped inside a body that seems more a hindrance than a help. But one day, God introduces us to the Lamb and something starts to bubble out of us that we never knew was there. We cannot worship in our own strength, but revelation of the Lamb draws a beauty out of us that we did not know ourselves capable of. If we want to come before "Him who sits upon the throne" to participate in heavenly worship, our journey also must to bring us face-to-face with the Cross, resurrection, and ascension of this glorious Lamb. This story, and none other, provokes such worship from sinful humanity.

The harp is the first item that the elders lay hold of, and it represents God-initiated, God-anointed, God-glorifying praise and worship. We sing to Him, and we sing to the world of Him; it is worship that witnesses, and a witness that worships. The song is so captivating that, in the end, multitudes from every nation on the earth will respond and find themselves also before the throne of grace.

In Heaven, the playing of these harps has a very dramatic effect. *"And I heard a sound from heaven like the roar of rushing waters and like a loud peal of thunder. The sound I heard was like that of harpists playing their harps"* (Rev. 14:2). Here, in Revelation 5, they provide glorious accompaniment to the Song of the Lamb, and do so in such a way that all Heaven erupts into a glorious praise heard throughout all the ends of the earth!

The Bowl

If the first item in the elders' hands is an instrument of worship, then the second is the golden bowl of prayer. *"Each one had a harp and they were holding golden bowls full of incense, which are the prayers of the saints"* (Rev. 5:8). This is a strange principle. The scroll is in the hands of the Lamb, and God's purposes will flourish in His hand. However, the Church has responsibility to pray that will into being. The Lamb has taught us what to pray: *"Our Father in heaven, hallowed be Your name, Your kingdom come, Your will be done on earth as it is in heaven"* (Matt. 6:9-10). So, we are charged to pray that the scroll's contents will be worked out in reality on the earth and in our lives.

The revelation of the Lamb makes priests out of the 24 elders (see Rev. 5:10). The scroll is in the hands of the Lamb; while worship and prayer are in the Church's hands. As the Lamb laid hold of the scroll, we also need to be purposeful in laying hold of tools God has placed into our hands. As we partner with Him in prayer and praise Him in song, we discover our crucial role in all that God is doing not just on the earth, but also in Heaven itself.

CHAPTER 5

The Liturgy of Heavenly Worship

The Five Songs of Revelation 4 and 5

In the previous chapters, we have been encouraged to "come up" and to take in sights that add fuel to our worship. We have had our eyes opened to the awesome throne where God sparkles and the Spirit blazes. We have been led on a journey to the center of heavenly worship where we find the all-conquering Lamb.

Now, we need to look at the songs ignited by this fuel. Five of them occur in Revelation 4 and 5, and they take us on their own journey. I am suggesting that these songs represent the progression of worship in Heaven from the first days of creation until the end of this present age, which culminates in the fulfillment of all God's purposes. This is not the only way to look at these Scriptures, but in working our way through these verses, I hope this approach will give a deeper understanding of heavenly worship's true nature.

My text for this chapter is based on a sermon that I wrote for a Sunday morning meeting, in which we went through Revelation 4 and 5. After reading the relevant passages for each song, we worshiped together and sang songs that carried the same heart as those within Revelation 4 and 5. This proved to be a powerful way of experiencing, to some small measure, what we see happening in Heaven.

So, let's look at each of these five songs, and see how they map out God's purposes through the ages—from creation to re-creation—and revolve around the Lamb's appearance in all His crucified and risen glory. Noticing who sings what songs and what the particular focus and themes are is of vital significance.

Song One: The Song of Creation (Rev. 4:6b-8)

There is some debate about what the four living creatures represent. Ezekiel sees such images and calls them cherubim (see Ezek. 10:14). These obviously mystical and wonderful heavenly beings have faces that "look like" those of earthly creatures. Therefore, it is possible that they stand before the throne and represent the beauty and diversity of God's creation, both in Heaven and on earth. If that is so, then there is a powerful truth here. The faces of recognizable, earthly creatures on heavenly beings suggest that a clear distinction does not exist between Heaven and earth after all. Looking at these creatures, we cannot clearly say, "This is of Heaven" or "This is of earth," because both appear to be true.

Perhaps, they prophetically represent what is yet to come. Revelation 21 gives stunning information that there will be a new earth and a new Heaven. This new Heaven and new earth will not be two separate entities, but will become one. The Creator of all things declares, *"I am making everything new!"* (Rev. 21:5), and everything means Heaven and earth! In that sense, these glorious creatures quite possibly represent the entirety of His creation—heavenly and earthly—operating in unity and harmony as a prophetic prototype of what is to come. That reminds us of the wonderful truth that we are heavenly and earthly creatures! Currently, those two realities seem to conflict as we wrestle to get rid of our old, earthly natures (see Rom. 7). But, in the end, the sons of God will be revealed for who they are, and all of creation stands on tiptoes waiting for that event! (See Romans 8:19 in *The Message*.)

Not only do these cherubim appear heavenly and earthly, but they can also cross over from one realm to the other in their role as the chariot of God. Psalm 18:10 tells us that God *"mounted the cherubim and flew; He soared on the wings of the wind."* Ezekiel sees them carrying the very throne of God (see Ezek. 1:25-26). These creatures—each with six wings and a multitude of eyes—are in constant adoration: *"Day and night they never stop saying..."* (Rev. 4:8b). This chorus has been repeated over and over, since the beginning of creation, and echoes alongside the never-ending song that God put into creation itself.

The heavens declare the glory of God; the skies proclaim the work of His hands. Day after day they pour forth speech; night after night they display knowledge. There is no speech or language where their voice is not heard. Their voice goes out into all the earth, their words to the ends of the earth (Psalm 19:1-4a).

God has created a universe that sings. The mighty mountains sing of splendor and majesty; the oceans and storms testify to power way beyond anything we can produce and it's totally outside of our control; while the sparrow sings worship to a God who shows intricate care and tenderness, even to those who are not so lovely. Jesus said that if we wouldn't worship, then *"the stones will cry out"* (Luke 19:40).

We are not the first worshipers in creation, but if we listen to what creation is saying, then we may join in its song! If we had eyes to see—as the four living creatures do—then we would constantly be in awe. Then, mankind would be without any excuse, because creation declares in booming tones of the glory of the One True God. Indeed, we are without excuse, because we all have eyes and senses. However, we humans would need to be covered with eyes— just as some of the angelic beings are—to even begin to take in all that He is.

These creatures are covered in eyes made to eternally gaze into the glories of God. Even with all those eyes, they will never become tired or bored; each glance will reveal some new wonder, even after an eternity of gazing. So, like creation from the beginning of time, the four living creatures never stop saying, "Holy! Holy! Holy!" That is a declaration of the transcendence of God. However glorious and wonderful they are, and however awesome creation is, God far, far, far exceeds them all.

When NASA's interstellar Hubble Telescope first sent back pictures of uncharted space, humanity was amazed at the universe's beauty and majesty. The vastness of planets, stars, and galaxies left mankind stunned, while the splendor of colors and shapes never before seen took their breath away. Yet, however huge and glorious the universe may be, it is still small in splendor when compared with the One who created it all. The heavenly creatures name Him: "The Lord God Almighty." He is the ruler over all creation, the one being from whom all others emanate, and is supreme in all power and authority. They say, "He was." Creation insists that there is a Creator—a Someone before the world came into being, who is the author of everything that exists.

The heavenly creatures say that, "He is." Creation also insists that there is a sustaining power, as well as a creative power. It is not as if God created everything, gave His creation a set of rules and laws on how to operate, and then sat back and watched. Of course, rules and laws govern the operation of our universe, but laws do not sustain it. Only God, who still spins stars in His hands and feeds sparrows, is the One who sustains. He lives, and, in so doing, He continues to be the life source of every living thing. He is provider, healer, protector, and savior. Nothing can exist without Him. The only reason that we breathe is because He gives us breath.

Finally, "He is to come." Creation lives in hope, despite its abuse suffered at the hands of men. Crocuses still come up out of recently frozen ground, and butterflies still blossom out of cocoons. New life continues to spring up and, as it does so, sings of a time when the Lord God Almighty will return and restore life in all its fullness to His creation. So, the living creatures declare in perpetual chorus: "Holy, Holy, Holy, is the Lord God Almighty who was and is and is to come."

Song Two: The Saints' Reply (Rev. 4:9-11)

Most commentators agree that the 24 elders represent the saints of the Old and New Testaments (that is, the 12 tribes of

Israel added to the 12 apostles of the Lamb). But how they are described is interesting. In Revelation 3, Jesus—the Head of the Church—confronts the Laodicean church as being "wretched, pitiful, poor, blind, and naked." In fact, unlike all the other churches He addresses, Jesus can find nothing positive to say about them.

Yet, to this sorry group of people He offers riches, white robes, and eye salve. His words are recorded as thus: *"I counsel you to buy from Me gold refined in the fire, so you can become rich; and white clothes to wear, so you can cover your shameful nakedness; and salve to put on your eyes so that you can see"* (Rev. 3:18). Even more incredibly, He gives an incredible promise to this most lukewarm church: *"To him who overcomes, I will give the right to sit with Me on My throne, just as I overcame and sat down with My Father on His throne"* (Rev. 3:21).

In the very next scene of John's heavenly vision, 24 elders are "dressed in white" with "crowns of gold on their heads," and, obviously, are face-to-face with the living God and seated on thrones surrounding The Throne. Here is an immediate, powerful image of the truth of God's promises. It's a wonderful picture of God's grace and mercy, and His amazing ability to take poor, wretched humanity and lift them up to become enthroned with Him in the highest place of the universe.

These 24 elders represent "overcomers" who simply persevered by faith and kept going. Here sit mighty men of God like Moses and Elijah. But here, too, sits the harlot Rahab and the adulterer and murderer David. Here sit great-grandparents, grandparents, mothers, fathers, and children taken from the earth before they had a chance to grow; all are now gloriously clothed, with rewards of sufferings on their heads, and are seated in the royal estate, while gazing into unending beauties of their God.

Again, we must not miss the obvious observation: The living creatures appear as a mixture of the heavenly and the earthly, and move easily between the two realms. But redeemed humanity is also in Heaven. We are heavenly creatures too! *"He has also set eternity in the hearts of men..."* (Eccles. 3:11). We were made for more than what this physical realm has to offer us. Redeemed man sits, sees, hears, and worships in Heaven. We will never be at home anywhere else.

So, here sits the universal Church in its regal attire. But, despite its privileged position, when the song of the four living creatures is heard, the people fall off their thrones. They aren't pushed, cajoled, or ordered—there simply is no other response to give. However, they do not fall *away* in fear and intimidation; they fall *before* the throne in awe and wonder, and then they "worship." What the living creatures are doing is not described here as worship (although it is in Rev. 7:11), but what comes from the hearts of the saints is!

They lay their crowns down before Him—even though the crowns represent God's reward to them for faithful perseverance through hardship, suffering, and persecution. Even that reward isn't worth keeping when presented with the overwhelming joy and satisfaction found in His presence. Then they worship. Notice that they don't speak before they are correctly postured. The knees are bowed and the crowns are removed before any sound comes from their lips. Heavenly worship has to do with knees and heads, before it has to do with tongues. They willingly lay aside even God-given privileges and get as low as they can before Him. This is not shallow or presumptuous worship; these are lives laid down in adoration—not just for this life—but for all eternity.

What these saints say appears to be a response to what is heard coming from the living creatures. In the natural realm, the eagles soar and the lions roar, and then mankind observes in wonder. Then, if he has eye salve, he looks beyond the natural to the source of all that exists—and then worships.

"O Lord my God, when I in awesome wonder

Consider all the works Thy hand hath made.

I see the stars; I hear the rolling thunder;

Thy power throughout the universe displayed.

Then sings my soul, my savior God to Thee,

'How great Thou art! How great Thou art!'

Then sings my soul, my savior God to Thee,

'How great Thou art! How great Thou art!'"

—*Stuart K. Hine (1953)*

Creation—as seen through the right eyes—provokes worship. So *"whenever" the creatures speak, the elders say, from the posture of greatest humility: "You are worthy, our Lord and God..."* (Rev. 4:11).

Unlike the living creatures, the elders claim a personal intimacy with Him who sits upon the throne—it's not *"The* Lord God Almighty" but *"Our* Lord and God." Also, notice that it's not personal intimacy (*"my* Lord and God"), but corporate intimacy (*"our* Lord and God"). Christianity is not an individualistic belief ("it's just about Jesus and me"); rather, it finds fullest expression, particularly in worship, through a corporate body of people.

Here, as in all the songs of Heaven recorded in this Revelation, there is no mention of "me" or "mine." Any remnant of self has been lost in the glory and majesty set before them. More than that, they sing one song, not lots of different styles of songs blended together. They sing as one man—worshiping together as the Body of Christ. We do need to develop our own life of personal worship with God, but that can never be an adequate alternative to worshiping together. This truth—as we will see when we come to the song of the Lamb—applies as much to individual churches as it does to individual saints. We cannot have the worship of Heaven if we will not worship together.

The elders go on to say: *"You are worthy, our Lord and God, to receive all honor and glory and power, for You created all things..."* (Rev. 4:11); and, therefore, everything belongs to Him. Nowadays, there is much discussion about land claims and rights, and God Himself has spoken about being careful not to move our neighbor's boundaries just to suit our own needs (see Deut. 27:17). To the Christian, however, *"The earth is the Lord's and everything in it, the world, and all who live in it; for He founded it upon the seas and established it upon the waters"* (Ps. 24:1-2). Not only that, but God created *all things*. However brilliant we might believe the human race to be, we cannot truly claim to have invented or created anything. What we have achieved has only been done because God gave us the ability to do it in the first place.

Creation came into being because God desired it: *"...and by Your will they* [all things] *were created..."* (Rev. 4:11). He desired His creation to be a source of joy and glory to Him, and so it will be in the end. We were all created because God wanted us to be. We are here because He desired that we should be born. Parents seek to conceive because they look forward to having children. God made us because He wanted us as His children. God willed us into being: *"by Your will they...have their being"* (Rev. 4:11). Nothing and no one can live without Him. To those who seek Him, He becomes the supply of everything that they need.

"For with you is the fountain of life" (Ps. 36:9). The people of Zion sing, *"All my fountains are in You"* (Ps. 87:7). So, the living creatures make their declaration to "Him who sits upon the throne," and that inspires the elders to respond with their own worship. The mixture of the two strains of praise and adoration is glorious, but the best is yet to come.

Song Three: The Song of the Lamb (Rev. 5:9-10)

The 24 elders represent members of a broken and sinful humanity who have somehow found their way into Heaven and the presence of Almighty God. How did they get there? That question is answered for us in Revelation 5.

A turning point in the liturgy of Heaven occurs when the scroll is brought out. Heavenly worship should always find its fuel in the Word of God. Representing the last will and testament of God for

His creation, the sealed document cannot be opened. No one has been found who is worthy enough. However, one of the elders informs us that there is Someone fully able to open the scroll, and also to deal with its consequences. Tears are wiped away as the central figure in this drama comes into view.

We see Jesus, the crucified Lamb of the Cross, who is still bearing His scars as He takes His stand in Heaven! At first, this sight is shocking in a Heaven that is supposed to be full of glory and joy. Here is a lamb that looks as if it has been violently slaughtered. Here, in the heart of the throne of God, is evidence of suffering and pain. The image is so captivating that, for a moment, attention gets drawn away from Him who sits upon the throne. Not only is our gaze distracted, but it appears as if our worship is diverted too. The 24 elders fall down before the Lamb, just as they had done to God on His throne. Far from being idolatry or blasphemy, this simple act illustrates what is possibly the Bible's greatest revelation; in fact, it could be the most wondrous truth of all time.

Bowing to this Lamb is, of course, not a threat to God the Father. When John the Baptist saw Jesus coming, he said, *"Look, the Lamb of God who takes away the sin of the world"* (John 1:29). The Father answered from Heaven with righteous pride, *"You are My Son, whom I love; with You I am well pleased"* (Luke 3:22). The Father receives immense pleasure from seeing the Lamb worshiped because this is His beloved Son! With all its scars of sacrifice, the Lamb is God, just as much as the awesome Being of unapproachable light who lives on the throne.

The elders standing in Heaven have made a journey from broken humanity to heavenly beings. Now, a new image—the Lamb—suggests a journey opposite from that of the elders. Here, for our sake, the Heavenly Being has become the most vulnerable of created beings. Suddenly, we are confronted with God's astonishing love, which is made plain to us by the two images of God set before us. Here we can see—in vivid, unforgettable terms—the distance that Almighty God has traveled on behalf of the rebellious sinful world that He so loves.

Seated on the throne is indescribable glory, and standing in the center of the throne is the essence of ordinariness. Here is priceless worth, and a creature of very little value. Here is one so full of splendor that you cannot fully behold Him, and yet so common that you wouldn't give Him more than a glance. Here is incredible power and strength, and also utter weakness. Here is a God who lives in unapproachable light, and a God so approachable that a child can sit on His knee. Here is a God who appears untouchable, and who invites you to touch Him, even if you are a leper or a prostitute.

Here is a God so touchable that you can push Him, hit Him, beat Him, or spit on Him. You can strip Him naked and laugh at Him. You can put spikes through His wrists and ankles, nail Him to a cross, and put a spear in His side. Having suffered all of that, He will still love you enough to open your eyes to see the truth. After all, the Roman centurion is the one whom God graced with eye salve to see who Jesus really was. When his eyes became opened, he responded in worship: *"And when the centurion, who stood there in front of Jesus, heard His cry and saw how He died, he said, 'Surely this man was the Son of God'"* (Mark 15:39); and *"The centurion, seeing what had happened, praised God"* (Luke 23:47).

The wounds of Jesus—inflicted on earth—are still visible in Heaven. These wounds are what make this God so compellingly attractive.

"Crown Him the Lord of love! Behold His hands and side,

Rich wounds, yet visible above, in beauty glorified.

No angel in the sky can fully bear that sight,

But downward bends his wond'ring eyes

At mysteries so bright."

—*Matthew Bridges (1854)*

The sight of those wounds opened Thomas' eyes to the truth of who this Lamb really was. He had followed Jesus for three years and had watched and heard incredible things. But only when Thomas had seen and touched those scars were his eyes fully opened and he exclaimed: *"My Lord and my God!"* (John 20:28). Here, in Revelation, the 24 elders take in the same sight as did Thomas and the centurion, and they respond in the same way. Falling down before the Lamb, as they had fallen down before "Him who sits upon the throne," they made the same declaration as Thomas: "My Lord and my God!"

The Lamb takes His stand "in the center of the throne." This is where He belongs—it is His by right! The Lamb stands in the center of the throne in Heaven, and, therefore, also at the center of all that is and ever shall be.

> *He is the image of the invisible God, the firstborn over all creation. For by Him all things were created: things in heaven and on earth, visible and invisible, whether thrones or powers or rulers or authorities; all things were created by Him and for Him. He is before all things, and in Him all things hold together. And He is the head of the body, the church; He is the beginning and the firstborn from among the dead, so that in everything He might have the supremacy. For God was pleased to have all His fullness dwell in Him, and through Him to reconcile to Himself all things, whether things on earth or things in heaven, by making peace through His blood, shed on the cross* (Colossians 1:15-20).

As an advocate before His throne, He stands between God and the elders to plead their case. This is how the sinners came to be here! They have put their trust in the most eloquent and persuasive of lawyers. Blood speaks louder than words at the throne of God, and Jesus poured out His own lifeblood so that we could stand with Him here!

He stands at the center of the throne so that He can orchestrate Heaven's worship. Heaven once had a worship leader whose heart became proud. His true motivation was revealed in his final temptation of Christ in the wilderness. *"All this I will give You...if You will bow down and worship me"* (Matt. 4:9). Realizing satan's problem was a sobering moment for me. Satan wasn't content just to be a worship leader; he wanted to be worshiped. As a result of his ambition and pride, he was cast down.

Now, Heaven has a new worship leader, a new Morning Star (see Rev. 22:16), who chose the path of humility and has been highly exalted. He was content to be a suffering servant and take the lowest place. As a result, not only does He lead worship in Heaven, but the Father has also made Him an object of worship.

Therefore God exalted Him to the highest place and gave Him the name above every name, that at the name of Jesus every knee should bow, in heaven and on earth and under the earth, and every tongue confess that Jesus Christ is Lord, to the glory of God the Father (Philippians 2:9-11).

He takes the scroll from the right hand of His Father; as He does so, we know now that there is no doubt as to history's outcome. He may appear as a weak Lamb, but closer inspection reveals Him as the Lion of Judah who carries all authority and power on His meek, lowly shoulders. The elders and the living creatures now have something fresh to sing about. And how they do sing!

Their previous declarations—made in Revelation 4—were spoken, but now John uses a different word in the Greek. This time, there is music and melody. There are three places in the Book of Revelation where this word for *sing* is used: Revelation 5:9; 14:3; and 15:3. Each time the song's focus is the same: The Lamb's emergence provokes singing in Heaven and it is the redeemed who lead the song. Why shouldn't they?

"Ransomed, healed, restored, forgiven,

Who, like thee, His praise should sing?"

—Henry F. Lyte (1834)

Something wonderful exists about the way we are made. We are often marked by pride and arrogance, but once broken by a revelation of the Lamb of God, a change occurs: A sweet, fragrant worship suddenly emerges from our hearts, and it cannot be matched by any other being in all creation, not even the angels! God has wanted to hear this song sung since before He created the earth; He wanted a beautiful sound in honor of the Son that He loves.

So, He created man and woman, both of whom have a God-given capacity to thrill His heart with worship and adoration like nothing else in all creation. The plain truth is that if we had not sinned and rebelled against God, and if Jesus did not die on the Cross, then we would not be able to sing as we do now. The entire master plan of sin and salvation is designed to produce this incredible, unique quality of worship.

So, the Lord puts a harp into our hands (see Rev. 15:2), and tells us to fill Heaven and earth with our music. He wants all of Heaven, earth, and creation to hear the glory of His Christ. We need to sing *to* Him in Heaven and sing *of* Him to the earth. Such singing cannot be coerced, conducted, or orchestrated. Our fourth child, Elizabeth, sometimes sits behind me when we are driving and spontaneously sings; she does so simply because she is so content and happy at having us all in the car together going somewhere. When we are content and happy, we don't have to be told to sing, hum, or whistle—it just flows out of us naturally. Such is the motivation for these elders. Content and gloriously happy at the revelation of the Lamb, the music just flows out of them naturally.

When doing lots of exhortation to encourage God's people into a place of worship, perhaps we need to be reminded that true worship flows very naturally out of hearts that are content and happy in Jesus. So, the elders sing. Again, let's not miss the obvious: The primary instrument of heavenly worship is the voice. Harps and trumpets appear at various points in the Book of Revelation, and other instruments may be playing, but the emphasis is always on the voice.

The elders sing a new song never before heard in all of creation or Heaven. Of the three times that this word for "sing" is mentioned in Revelation, it twice refers to a "new song" (Rev. 5:9 and 14:3), and once to an old one (the song of Moses recorded in Rev. 15:3). Heavenly worship includes both the old and the new. This new song sets all of Heaven singing, and it comes from the *Church. This is the Song of the Lamb: "You are worthy to take the scroll and to open its seals because You were slain..."* (Rev. 5:9). What a stunning statement!

The elders and the living creatures worship Him who sits on the throne because He is the source of all life. Now, they are singing to the Lamb because He gave up His life for us all. The Father lives and gives life. The Son dies and gives life! But—because He was willing to die in order to please His Father—He is worthy to handle the will of God. The Father knows that He can trust Jesus with everything: *"...and with Your blood, You purchased men for God..."* (Rev. 4:9). The Lamb is worthy because He has bought a very precious gift to present to His Father. He paid for it in a currency that is priceless: His own blood. He did it for the joy that was set before Him (see Heb. 12:2).

I am sure that the Lamb gets great joy from seeing people saved, healed, and set free, but that is not His greatest joy. The foremost joy set before Jesus when facing the Cross was to see the pleased smile on His Father's face when presenting Him with the fruit of His sufferings. He did it for His Father first, not for me, or even the millions of people He has saved over the centuries. To please His Father, Jesus brought Him the one gift that would give His Father the greatest pleasure. The elders themselves represent that gift, and all of us bought with the blood of Jesus are also part of that gift; we have all been purchased by a Son who wants to see His Father both glorified and satisfied.

Seemingly, the elders are satisfied simply to be the gift. They could have sung, "For You were slain and with Your blood You purified us, You provided for us, You made a way into Heaven for us...." But while watching this wonderful exchange between Father and Son, they are not thinking about what they are receiving from this. Reveling in the relationship before them, they are content with the role as a love offering from one to the other. Our greatest pleasure in Heaven, I believe, will be to see the Father's love for His Son, and the love that Jesus has for His Father, and to know that we contributed to that love's fulfillment.

What makes this gift special? First of all, it represents the return of God's children. Unlike the prodigal son's older brother, Jesus went searching for His distraught Father's wandering sons and daughters and brought them home to Him.

Second, it is a *people*, not just a collection of individuals. This is God's family. When Adam needed a family, God gently put him into a deep sleep and painlessly took a rib from his side. Then He handcrafted Eve and brought her to Adam. When God needed a family, He allowed man to take the second Adam—Jesus—and cruelly put Him into a deeper sleep. In the process, they also pierced His side and drew out all His lifeblood. Yet, that blood has fashioned the most wonderful Bride for His Son and the most glorious of families for the Father.

Third, this gift is made special by its incredible variety: *"from every tribe and language and people and nation"* (Rev. 5:9).

Fourth, it gives the Father a kingdom (see Rev. 4:10). The problem with Israel's pestering Samuel for a king was not so much that it was wrong to have a king; the real issue was that they already had one! When Samuel went to the Lord, His response was, *"it is not you they have rejected, but they have rejected Me as their King"* (1 Sam. 8:7). However, God did not stop being a King just because His people rejected Him. In the very next generation, He began to take back the Kingdom for Himself. David's throne was His throne and David's worship leaders knew it! *"How awesome is the Lord most high, the great King over all the earth"* (Ps. 47:2). Now, after the Cross and resurrection, the Kingdom is restored to its rightful King. The people—as represented by the elders—rejoice in that restoration.

Fifth, it gives God a permanent priesthood (see Rev. 4:10). Through the prophet Jeremiah, God made a solemn promise to His people: *"David will never fail to have a man sit on the throne of the house of Israel, nor will the priests, who are Levites, ever fail to have a man stand before Me continually to offer burnt offerings, to burn grain offerings and to present sacrifices"* (Jer. 33:17).

That Scripture obviously refers to Christ, who has a permanent priesthood before the throne of God. In the same prophecy, however, God later expands this thought so that it incorporates the Abramic covenant: *"I will make the descendants of David My servant and the Levites who minister before Me as countless as the stars of the sky and as measureless as the sand on the seashore"* (Jer. 33:22). Not only does Jesus have a permanent royal priesthood, but so do we as His people. This is an important perspective about heavenly worship: Not only will we have eternal joys and pleasures at His right hand, but together with His Son, we also have the privilege of bringing Him eternal joy and pleasure.

Finally, the gift that Jesus gives to His Father brings perfect and complete restoration to God's original plan for creation. This gift will perfectly fulfill the requirements of God's original blessing to Adam and Eve of having dominion over all that He has made; "they will reign on the earth." In Revelation, we see all of God's plans, covenants, and promises made since before the first day of creation become completely fulfilled. All of this is done through a meek, lowly Lamb and a Cross of wood. That such a seemingly complex problem could have a simple solution is truly incredible. That one act—and the life and grace that flowed from it—bought for the Father in Heaven all that His heart desired. We are now that gift. Standing today, while washed in the blood of the Lamb, we bring Him immense pleasure.

So the 24 elders sing a new song, and it is only one song! They are from *"every tribe and language and people and nation"* (Rev. 5:9), but they sing one song! This is true heavenly worship. It comes from hearts reconciled by the blood of the Lamb and reconciled to God and to each other. This blending of voices of the nations in worship is precisely what makes heavenly worship so special. By inference, we cannot truly have this level of worship if we do not worship together across boundaries of nationality, culture, and language. Today, such unity happens in encouraging ways in many parts of the world. However, we still struggle to worship with believers from our own nation, and even those who fellowship down the street from us. If we do not cross these boundaries, then we are not giving the Father the worship that Jesus died for.

If we want to grow in our own expressions of worship as individuals, then—before writing new songs, or even having extended times of personally seeking the Lord—we may need to learn to sing the song of the Lamb together! Perhaps we need to lose self-absorption, or that sense of "me" and "mine" discussed earlier in this chapter. The Son has given His Father a wonderful gift, and we are that gift. So, let us pick up our harps and join our brothers and sisters who have gone before us, as well as those currently alive on the earth. Together with the elders, let us fill Heaven and earth with the sound of "The Song of the Lamb." When we do this together, the impact will be astounding.

Song Four: The Angelic Chorus (Rev. 5:12)

The elders and living creatures begin to sing this new song, and it sets all of Heaven to singing! Encircling the throne is a huge angelic chorus that is *"numbering thousands upon thousands, and ten thousand times ten thousand"* (Rev. 5:11). They cannot sing what the redeemed can sing. Why is that? Because they cannot fully appreciate God's mercy and salvation in the way that a saved sinner can. But their voices do beautifully complement the new melody. We have not noticed them before—as they have been more than content to stay in the background. But, now, they take their place in increasing the circle of worship around the throne. What began in Revelation 4 with a group of 4 and then 24, now numbers in the hundreds of thousands as the angelic hosts join in.

These are not the traditionally overweight cherubs who sit on clouds with harps in their hands; these are glorious, mighty spiritual beings. Their volume must be beyond anything we have ever heard upon the earth. This cannot be compared to rock concerts or the unison singing of a European soccer stadium crowd. Hundreds of thousands of mighty warrior angels sing out "in a loud voice," and that sound must shake all of creation. Besides adding volume, they add tremendous strength; they surround the living creatures and the 24 elders and hem them into the very presence of God.

Interestingly, John has gone back to the Greek word he used for "sing" in Revelation 4; this definition is a loud chant or shout, rather than a tuneful melody. It appears that the sweetest sounds of worship still come from saved humanity, and these sounds are even sweeter than angelic voices. So, as the angels hear our praise, they come behind us to add power and strength to our worship and to press us into the Lamb and our God upon His throne.

These angels had, of course, a choice to do otherwise. But they chose to ignore the foolish arrogance of their fellow angel, lucifer, and wait for the greatest worship leader to be lifted up. These loyal ones scorned personal ambition and pride to maintain their privileged position around the throne. Truly worshiping God with pride in our hearts is impossible. The devil's "I will arise" attitude precipitated the God response of "You will fall away from My presence forever!" But the Lamb's "I will descend" attitude precipitates His Father's response of "I will lift You up and give You the highest place." The way to "come up" and meet with God is to humble ourselves before Him.

At the end of the age, this is the only sort of worship that will remain.

From beyond the rivers of Cush, My worshipers, My scattered people, will bring Me offerings...I will remove from this city those who rejoice in their pride. Never again will you be haughty on My holy hill. But I will leave within you the meek and humble, who trust in the name of the Lord (Zephaniah 3:10-12).

It's interesting that there is no mention of the devil, demons, or evil in either of these two chapters; the themes are too holy and glorious to be stained with such thoughts. The strong implication is that—despite the obvious damage that these forces can do—they have no real effect on the ultimate outcome. So, they don't even bear mentioning when it comes to worship of the Lamb and Him who sits upon the throne. Worship of Heaven will continue, regardless of any scheme that satan can produce. The working out of God's will—as represented by the scroll in the Lamb's hands—is so certain that the forces of darkness are practically irrelevant. Whatever depth of evil and depravity we see in the Book of Revelation's next few chapters, remember that the end is already secured in Christ, and it concerns a spectacular, glorious worship.

So the angels join in the song of the Lamb, expand on the theme of the saints, and underscore His new place of glory in Heaven. He who once was *"made a little lower than the angels"* (Heb. 2:7) is now high above them, and they are thrilled at His exaltation! *"Worthy is the Lamb who was slain, to receive power and wealth and wisdom and strength and honor and glory and praise"* (Rev. 5:12). There is no "because" since no reason is necessary; the Lamb's worthiness is ultimately explained by the scars that He bears, the millions of saved sinners that bow before Him, and the incredible pleasure that He has brought to His Father.

Song Five: The Climax of All Things! (Rev. 5:13)

So, through the ages, the worship has grown and grown. It starts with declarations of the living creatures and the elders' response to the creatures' message, and then rises to new heights as the crucified Lamb takes His place before the throne as both worship leader and object of worship. Now, a new melody takes over. The Song of the Lamb is added to the worship of "Him who sits upon the throne," and Heaven explodes into majestic music as thousands upon thousands of angels join the chorus of the saints. However, more is yet to come.

The Song of the Lamb is so compelling in its theme, that it's like a Pied Piper gathering thousands and thousands of devoted followers in its wake. The worship of the Church gloriously affects and changes the worship of Heaven. However, our worship is not for Heaven alone. Written in the scroll is the Father's expressed will that all ends of the earth shall hear this song because He desires knowledge of His glory to cover the earth just as waters cover the sea (see Hab. 2:14).

True heavenly worship cannot be fully developed within the four walls of our churches alone, and in no way can it be divorced from evangelism. The Song of the Lamb is to be sung to the ends of the earth before the end will come. It could be "sung" with instruments or a melody or, more often, by the simple sharing of a testimony or a loaf of bread, or through a life that radiates Jesus' love, or by the preaching of the gospel.

The whole earth needs to hear of Christ's glory, and the good news of salvation that can be found in Him alone. The end result will be utterly beyond anything to be grasped by the human imagination—even in our wildest dreams. John records it this way: *"Then I heard every creature in heaven and on earth and under the earth and on the sea and all that is in them singing"* (Rev. 5:13).

Is this real, or is it prophetic hyperbole? To those who wanted to stop His followers from praising Him, Jesus said, *"I tell you...if they keep quiet, the stones will cry out"* (Luke 19:40). Was He stretching the truth to make a point, or does creation have such a pent-up passion for worship that it will explode into highest praise if given the right catalyst? The Psalmists seemed to believe so! The writer of Psalm 148 obviously had enough eye salve to perceive what John was seeing in Revelation 5.

Praise the Lord. Praise the Lord from the heavens, praise Him in the heights above. Praise Him, all His angels, praise Him, all His heavenly hosts. Praise Him, sun and moon, praise Him, all you shining stars. Praise Him, you highest heavens and you waters above the skies. Let them praise the name of the Lord, for He commanded and they were created. He set them in place for ever and ever; He gave a decree that will never pass away. Praise the Lord from the earth, you great sea creatures and all ocean depths, lightning and hail, snow and clouds, stormy winds that do His bidding, you mountains and all hills, fruit trees and all cedars, wild animals and all cattle, small creatures and flying birds...Let them praise the name of the Lord, for His name alone is exalted; His splendor is above the earth and the heavens (Psalm 148:1-10,13).

The saints have been singing of a re-creation and the angels have joined in. Now, the old creation catches up; it has been waiting, even groaning for the sons of God to be revealed (see Rom. 8:19,22) because they will herald the re-creation to come. Creation watched Jesus rise from the dead and rejoiced about the broken curse and the starting restoration process. Now, creation hears the children of God in full chorus. At last, it's freed from bondage to death and decay and released to sing with all its recreated strength and vigor. Add the 4 living creatures, the 24 elders (who represent millions of saints), and the hundreds of thousands of angels, and we have countless different species of animal, bird, insect, and fish—in fact, every creature that exists.

The climax of the Book of Psalms is the climax of all God's purposes: *"Let everything that has breath praise the Lord"* (Ps. 150:6). As creation joins the symphony, total harmony occurs between Heaven and earth. They combine the focuses of the first four songs into one song; we have had two songs "to Him who sits upon the throne" in Revelation 4, as followed by two songs "to the lamb" in Revelation 5. Now, every creature in Heaven and earth, and under the earth, joins in singing to them both: *"To Him who sits upon the throne and to the Lamb be praise and honor and glory and power, for ever and ever"* (Rev. 5:13). In essence, they cry out: "Let there be eternal honor, everlasting glory, and never-ending power to Him who sits upon the throne and to the Lamb. And let the praise never end; let worship go on forever and ever!"

Witnessing this incredible scene of all-embracing cosmic worship, the four living creatures say "Amen!" In other words, "This is the way it should be!" The Church—having heard what has happened as a result of its worship both in Heaven and upon the earth—falls down for the third time and worships in awesome wonder, love, and praise! It will surely happen! It has been in the heart of God since before the ages of the earth. What an incredible hope! After all, what greater purpose can there be than to worship and witness here on earth that we have the joy of seeing many others in a joyful chorus, all because of our testimony!

The amazing fact is that we can hasten the day! The more we worship and witness here on earth, the sooner we will all join in worship with angels, archangels, and all of creation. There is no greater reason to live! Heavenly worship is the God-ordained destiny of all His saints, but we don't have to wait for death before participating. The door is open now, and the invitation is there for us all to "come up." Once there, we don't have to initiate our own worship experience but can simply flow with what is already happening. As we join in Heaven's worship, we will become more passionate about hastening its inevitable and glorious climax: the eternal, thunderous, cosmic worship of our Father in Heaven and His glorious Son.

"Lord Jesus, we come to You and ask for eye salve, so that we may see what is to come, and that, in seeing, we may find fresh vision and passion to pursue the glory of God in every nation and through all of creation. Come, Lord Jesus. We long for the day!"

CHAPTER 6

The Pinnacle of Heavenly Worship

⤝⚬⤞

Heaven is alive with the sound of glorious adoration, which has cascaded over into creation. Now every creature remaining in the seen and the unseen world sings with God-given might, "To Him who sits upon the throne and to the Lamb." The praise will go on forever and will never end. Surely, nothing more needs to be said. However, the last word on worship does not belong to creatures of earth and sky, nor to the saints and angels, and not even to the mighty cherubim. As in all things, the last word on heavenly worship belongs to the Lamb.

Given our study of Revelation 4 and 5, you would be forgiven for asking, "Well then, where are the Lamb's words on worship in these verses? The Lamb never says anything here, does He?" Oh, yes, He does! He speaks, and His actions speak louder than words. With these actions, He worships, and the sound of His song is what makes everyone else sing. His worship is the pinnacle of all worship, and it's the greatest worship ever presented before His Father's throne.

Where then is this worship recorded? It doesn't appear in Revelation 4 and 5. You need fresh eye salve to see it because it's not obvious at first. The answer is recorded for us in half a sentence in Revelation 5:6: *"then I saw a Lamb, looking as if it had been slain."* That doesn't sound like the last word on heavenly worship, but it is! The greatest part of the worship service in Heaven is an act, not a song. This one act actually gives meaning and voice to all the other songs. That point should not be lost on us.

Worship, as first introduced in the Bible, does not deal with either songs or music; rather, it is an act. As Abraham journeys towards the mountain, he tells his servants what he is about to do with Isaac: *"Stay here with the donkey while I and the boy go over there. We will worship..."* (Gen. 22:5). He was not going up the mountain to sing songs, but to sacrifice his son. This was to be an act of worship—a song without words or music.

When God called His people out of Egypt, He did so with the express purpose of teaching them to worship Him. However, He did not begin by teaching them songs but by giving them instructions on how to act so as to worship Him. In giving them the Law and all the instructions for the tabernacle and the priesthood, He taught them to worship Him without singing. Here are even more songs without words or music.

It's not that God doesn't want songs. Moses wrote one that is still being sung in the liturgy of Heaven (see Rev. 15:3). Many songs of worship exist in the Bible, but biblical worship did not begin with a song, but with an action. The pinnacle of heavenly worship is also not a song—even though it's surrounded in the text by the best songs of all—it is an action. Jesus' worship had total authenticity because He showed it through the way that He lived, not the songs that He sang. In fact, not much can be said about Jesus' worship through song while He was on the earth; this is a startling omission given the importance that singing plays in biblical worship.

Scripture records one instance of His singing a hymn with His disciples (see Matt. 26:30; Mark 14:26). But there is no record of Jesus singing by Himself, although I am sure that He did. In addition, as far as we know, He wrote no worship songs. For if He had, surely someone would have written them down so that the Church could sing them. There may not be much recorded of Jesus worshiping in song, but His whole life, and certainly His death, was a wonderful worship song, and it's the greatest one ever written.

We live in an age where worshiping God in music has become big business; so much so that even non-Christian organizations are investing, with the intention of cashing in on its profits. Many cities (certainly in North America) have access to Christian radio stations that play worship music 24 hours a day. A single worship song that becomes popular can generate hundreds of thousands of dollars. Writers of such songs have become well-known all over the earth.

Such an atmosphere need not be a threat to true worship; in fact it could be part of God's stated desire that the earth be filled with knowledge of His glory as the waters cover the sea (see Hab. 2:14). However, this concentration on worship music can fuel the misconception that we only worship when we sing. This is a good time to remind ourselves that the Bible's greatest acts of worship (by Abraham and Jesus) were actions, and not songs. You could easily argue that the same is true today, and that the greatest worship comes from those who actively lay down their lives for the gospel.

This is not to diminish what is happening in the Christian music scene. Personally, I believe that in these days God is rebuilding David's fallen tabernacle and fulfilling Amos' prophetic declaration (see Amos 9:11-12) that James reiterated to apostles and elders in Jerusalem (see Acts 15:16-18). Fulfillment of this promise would include restoration of magnificent worship with the aim that nations be drawn to God's glory.

This was the focus of David's tabernacle as outlined in the song of dedication that he wrote: *"Give thanks to the Lord, call on His name; make known among the nations what He has done"* (1 Chron. 16:8). James also focused on this when he spoke to the council in Jerusalem, *"that the remnant of men may seek the Lord, and all the Gentiles who bear My name, says the Lord..."* (Acts 15:17). Men and women who are writing songs for nations to sing are blessing us all and pleasing the Father's heart, so they need our prayers, encouragement, and support. But many of them would be the first to say that worship is not only about music.

Revelation 5:6 is the last word on worship because it's the last word on every vital ingredient that makes up perfect worship—even though it doesn't include any singing. What are those ingredients? If we can uncover what they are, then it will surely help us to grow in our worship. Many ingredients are involved, but they can be gathered together under two main headings. Jesus' offering is the last word on worship because it's the last word on submission and sacrifice. As we shall see, these are the two main ingredients of heavenly worship.

The Last Word on Submission

When looking at the Lamb in Heaven, we first note His submission. As we shall see, this is the beginning of heavenly worship. This act was not self-motivated or self-initiated; Jesus was not trying to think of what song might please His Father the most. His Father actually told Jesus how to worship Him, and He received Jesus' subsequent act of obedience as the greatest worship He had ever been offered. This act, however, would cost the Son everything.

When Rachel, our third daughter, was nearly three years old she had to go into the hospital to have tubes put in her ears. It was a one-day surgery, so early that morning we went through all the preparations of getting her ready for her small operation. After a short time of waiting, we were asked to move to the operating area's entrance, where a nurse came to take Rachel's hand and lead her off to the waiting surgeon.

Our little daughter seemed to be coping quite well with it all. When the nurse came, Rachel gave me a kiss, clasped the nurse's hand, and allowed herself to be led through large, swinging doors into the operating room. Although Rachel was okay, I was struggling to hold my emotions together. That was one of those moments I will remember for the rest of my life. The surgeon, of course, could be trusted to do a good job, and the trained staff had done many successful operations before. But those facts did nothing to quell my anxiety.

When the Father asked His Son to walk through the gates of Heaven to come to earth, He put His Beloved's life in our hands. The Father knew that we couldn't be trusted to look after Him properly, and so did the Son. Jesus knew the pain and suffering that awaited Him, but His Father wanted this act of worship, so Jesus submitted Himself to His Father's will.

Hundreds of years before, God had been just as prescriptive with His people—the Israelites—about how He wanted them to worship Him. God took His people out of Egypt into the wilderness with Moses *"so that they might worship Me"* (Exod. 9:13). He brought them to the mountain and gave them strict instructions as to how they should worship Him. The instructions for worship, as given to Moses on Mount Sinai, can be put into two categories: One had to do with the tabernacle, the priestly functions, the sacrifices, and feasts; and the other had to do with the way they should live, which included the Ten Commandments and all its rules and regulations. The important point here is that—as with Jesus—the worship was not self-initiated or self-motivated. God did not tell them to write their own songs and come up with their own forms of worship. He was very prescriptive about what He wanted them to do.

Our desire to self-initiate is closely entangled with a warped, broken concept of self-worth. We can easily feel that we are only worth what we have to offer. This can be true of us as Christians when we come to worship. If we cannot think of what to say, pray, or do, or if we feel that we have nothing to give, then we often struggle with feelings of guilt, shame, and a sense that our worship is worthless. On the contrary, when we feel that we have plenty to say, pray, do, or have much to give, then our sense of guilt, shame, and worthlessness can be lifted (although it is not fully removed). In that case, we feel justified that our worship has some worth and merit.

Those views are seriously wrong, both theologically and doctrinally, and can leave people who genuinely want to worship God with a false sense of either contentment or inadequacy about their worship offerings. Both views are based on a concept of worship that is self-motivated and self-initiated. We believe that it is our job to come up with something pleasing and good enough for God. But Jesus did not approach worshiping His Father this way. Rather than looking inside Himself for some gift to bring, Jesus found out from His Father what worship would most bless Him. Worship of God does not begin in the heart of the worshiper. God is not looking for us to come up with worthwhile worship out of our own imagination. He is looking for us to listen to what He would like us to do, and then obey Him.

I enjoy writing worship songs, but after many years of trying, it's clear that I cannot come up with a great worship song by myself; it has to come from inspiration, not just perspiration. That does not mean that songwriting is not hard work, because it is. The inspiration often begins with a single lyric or tune, and then must go through a necessary "birthing" period where the song takes shape through hours of wrestling, praying, and struggling; sometimes, it even needs outside help from others to be fully brought to birth.

Jesus had a good understanding of what His Father desired in worship, but then He had to struggle His way through (especially in Gethsemane) to bring it to birth. His struggle, however, was not to find some deeper well of worship within Himself; His struggle was to find His way—through surrender—into His Father's will and resources so as to bring His act of worship to perfection.

A struggle in songwriting should be a struggle not so much in our abilities and experience (although God can and does use both), but a further wrestling into God's resources and heart for what He wants this song to be. In other words, the process is not self-initiated and self-motivated. Our songs can appear self-motivated, especially when they come out of the cries of our own hearts (like many of the Psalms) or out of circumstances we are going through. However, God brought those circumstances into our lives; God put those heart cries in us; and God wrung those heart cries out of us by allowing those circumstances to squeeze the songs into existence.

God clearly laid out for the Israelites how He wanted them to worship Him. They didn't feel any pressure of having to figure out how to put on a good worship service for God, and neither should we. As humans, we could never obey those clearly laid out instructions, but Jesus did when He came to earth, walked among us without sin, and then went to the Cross. By fully submitting Himself to what His Father wanted, Jesus fulfilled all the requirements for perfect worship—once and for all.

To put this concept into a family context, as parents we would all rather have obedience than nice singing. Every now and then, our girls like to put on shows for us. They disappear into some room and tell us that we can't enter. Then they dress up and practice their dances, songs, and jokes before announcing that we can come in and enjoy the creative delights that they have prepared for us. All of it is a lot of fun and brings a good deal of pleasure to Julia and I. However, that pleasure does not compare to what we feel when one of our girls—when faced with the prospect of doing what they don't like to do—says, "Yes, Mom" or "Yes, Dad," without any hint of bitterness. But, even that does not satisfy when compared with the feeling of seeing one of our girls saying "Yes" to Jesus. Singing can be wonderful, and God receives and enjoys such worship. But the greatest of all worship comes when actions match the song.

The writer to the Hebrews tells us how Jesus came to earth:

Therefore, when Christ came into the world, He said: "Sacrifice and offering You did not desire, but a body You prepared for Me; with burnt offerings and sin offerings You were not pleased. Then I said, "Here I am—it is written about Me in the scroll—I have come to do Your will, O God" (Hebrews 10:5-7).

Jesus didn't come merely to sing songs; He came to offer perfect worship, and that meant total submission.

Our Perfect Worship

We can also participate in perfect worship—not by getting the right songs on the set list, or by trying to live a perfect life of obedience—but simply by submitting ourselves to God's prescribed method of worshiping Him, which is through His Son. We need to begin by understanding that we cannot please God by trying to worship in and of ourselves. The perfect worship of Christ is what pleases the Father. If we want to please Him, then we need to receive by faith the worship of Jesus on the Cross as our worship, as opposed to bringing our own offering.

This seems simple enough, but it's very difficult for us to submit to. A drive within us wants to do something, or be someone, that is good enough for God. But all our righteousness is as filthy rags. Right living comes by accepting that only Jesus lived right, and then receiving by faith the gift of His righteousness for ourselves. Perfect worship comes by accepting that only Jesus worshiped perfectly, and then receiving His gift of perfect worship as our own.

The worship of Christ cannot be made more perfect; it has perfected praise before the Father once and for all. Whatever we then bring—in word, song, or deed—is offered to God, not to try to please Him with our own offering, nor to try to add to what Jesus did through His life and death. What pleases God is when we submit to His prescription for true worship, when we live, act, and sing by faith in what His glorious Son has already done. With that understanding, when we worship by faith in Jesus' act of perfect worship, then every offering we bring is perfected in Christ before the throne of God. We need never fear the Father's disappointment or disapproval. Our heavenly Father receives our worship as if Jesus is worshiping—because in fact, He is.

> *We do have such a High Priest* [One who can lead His people in perfect worship], *who sat down at the right hand of the throne of the Majesty in heaven, and who serves* [Greek "leitourgos," or, literally, the leader of the worship] *in the sanctuary, the true tabernacle set up by the Lord, not by man* (Hebrews 8:1-2).

Certain parts of the Body of Christ have an idea that you can "miss" it in worship. This is a tremendous pressure to many worship leaders, and one often unfortunately propagated by the way that Church leadership speaks about worship. The only way you can "miss" in worship is to not offer it in faith in Christ's perfect act of worship, or, in other words, to offer self-motivated and self-initiated worship.

I do believe that it's possible for a congregation to miss out on an experience of intimacy and closeness with God because worship leaders pick the wrong songs or take a wrong turn in leading a meeting. However, this must never be confused with what God has received through that worship. If offered in faith in Christ, then, by the time it reaches the Father's ears—wrong songs, wrong choices, and all—it has become perfect worship through Christ. This is the glory and wonder of justification. If someone says that is not true, then they are saying that Jesus' offering on the Cross was not enough for perfect worship and it needs to be added to. In its strongest terms, such a doctrine is a works-based heresy, yet it has quietly crept into how many of us see our worship.

We never could, and never can, offer anything to God purely of ourselves that can "make the grade" in worship. Jesus did it all, and when He did so, He did it for me as well as for Himself. His worship cannot be bettered or added to; we can merely participate and own it as ours through faith. If our worship is not offered in faith (and you can often tell by observing how much tension and strain we are under before, during, and after a worship time), then we need to get our eyes off ourselves and our own inadequacies, and get them back onto His perfect adequacy and finished work on the Cross. In the words of the writer to the Hebrews: *"Through Jesus, therefore, let us continually offer to God a sacrifice of praise—the fruit of lips that confess His name"* (Heb. 13:15).

When we talk about being unable to add to the perfect worship of Jesus on the Cross, we are speaking of the quality of worship. We cannot add a single note to the perfection of Jesus' worship.

However, by His grace, God is in the business of adding to the quantity of that worship. In that sense, the full symphony of perfect worship cannot be heard until the fullness of the Cross is brought to completion. That cannot happen until the last member of Heaven's choir has been brought in, and God declares the choir is complete and that it's time to bring matters on earth to a close. Jesus' act of worship on the Cross was perfect worship. But that act is being filled to all fullness by the gospel being preached across the earth, and the full harvest of saved sinners. If we can participate in bringing worship of Jesus on the Cross to its fullness, then we are increasing heavenly worship.

We know that God loves to be worshiped in psalms, hymns, and spiritual songs, and that He wants His people to always make melodies in their heart to Him (see Eph. 5:19). However, making a lasting contribution to Jesus' perfect worship is best done by participating in saving souls rather than in savoring songs. That is one way God has prescribed for us to worship Him. If we want to worship like Jesus, then we also need to submit to the Father's stated desire for how He wants us to worship Him. His submission in Gethsemane was crucial to the completion of Jesus' perfect act of worship: "Not My will but Yours" is where worship is perfected.

How do we submit in worship? We submit in worship when we first admit that we cannot bring God anything of ourselves that will please Him. Instead, we must choose to join in the song that was already perfected by the Lamb. This does not mean that we do not write and sing songs. Of course, such things bless the Father's heart, but only where offered through Jesus by the Spirit, rather than out of our own personal well of worship. Second, we submit in worship when we choose to participate in God's plan for how perfect heavenly worship should look. We do this by being personally involved in the Church's mission, which is to increase the size and variety of Heaven's choir to bring worship of Jesus to its fullness.

If we want to worship like Jesus, we need to submit to worshiping through Jesus and in Jesus. We can pray similar to how Jesus prayed in Gethsemane: "Not what I want in worship, Father, but what You want. Not what I want to bring You, but what You want me to bring. My worship doesn't begin in me; it begins in You. Lord, not my will in worship, but Yours."

The Last Word on Sacrifice

If the life and death of Jesus, the Lamb of God, was the last word on submission, then it was also the last word on sacrifice—one naturally leads to the other. Submission begins with an act of surrender and leads inevitably to servanthood. But this is not the servanthood of a waiter or a deacon, it is the servanthood of a *"doulos,"* or someone who has given up all rights and pledged themselves to the Master for life. That sort of servanthood demands a degree of selflessness that most of us have never experienced. Such selflessness in a sinful and fallen world inevitably leads to suffering, and suffering leads to sacrifice.

Surrender, submission, servanthood, selflessness, suffering, and sacrifice—these are the heart attitudes that perfected the worship of Jesus. These are all underscored in Paul's recording of Jesus' journey in worship, as found in Philippians 2:6-8:

> *Who, being in very nature God, did not consider equality with God something to be grasped* [surrender and submission], *but made Himself nothing* [selflessness, empty of self], *taking the very nature of a servant* [servanthood], *and being made in human likeness. And being found in appearance as a man, He humbled Himself and became obedient to death—even death on a cross!* [suffering and sacrifice]

The apostle Paul encourages us to go on a similar journey in worship: *"Your attitude should be the same as that of Christ Jesus"* (Phil. 2:5). Such a journey will always lead to sacrifice.

Abraham, under the inspiration and enabling of the Holy Spirit, set mankind a good example of what it means to worship God. Recognizing the need for submission, he did not come up with his own idea of what might please God. The Lord initiated the act of worship by asking Abraham to do something that Abraham himself would never have wanted to do. Abraham submitted to God's request for worship by instantly and completely setting out to obey what God wanted. "Early the next morning," Abraham got ready and set off for the region of Moriah (see Gen. 22:3).

For Abraham, however, the heart of submission and obedience in itself did not constitute worship. He did not tell his servants that he was worshiping as he went up the mountain to work out his act of obedience to God. Abraham told his servants that he would worship when he got to the place where God wanted him to go. In his mind, he would worship when he completed the task that God had asked of him. The completion of that task involved what was, for Abraham, the ultimate act of sacrifice. He was asked to kill his only son, Isaac, in whom he thought was hidden all the riches of God's promises for his life.

Therefore, when we ask how to give God the ultimate in worship, it's reasonable to assume that it requires our greatest sacrifice. For that reason, many of us have resigned ourselves to the belief that we could simply never do what Abraham did, and, therefore, are doomed to offer God what is, at best, second-rate worship while on this earth. However, inadequate theology is what leaves us in such a state. When Christ offered up Himself as a sacrifice for us, His ultimate act of worship fulfilled all the sacrificial acts of worship before and after that moment on the Cross of Calvary.

So, as with submission, we can participate in perfect sacrifice in worship by appropriating Jesus' worship by faith. Therefore, we are released from the burden of feeling that we never give enough of ourselves. Once again, we cannot add to the *quality* of the perfect sacrificial worship of Jesus, but we can contribute to its *quantity*. In other words, we can be part of its fullness.

Jesus suffered, and His suffering was His worship. However, there is a fullness to Jesus' suffering yet to be totally realized. The suffering Church adds to the worship of Jesus by filling up His Body with the full measure of His sufferings. Participating in such worship was a tremendous privilege for early Christians, and they encouraged each other in it. Here are some of their writings:

Now if we are children, then we are heirs...and co-heirs with Christ, [and what marks a child of God and a co-heir with Christ?] if indeed we share in His sufferings in order that we may also share in His glory (Romans 8:17).

For just as the sufferings of Christ flow over into our lives, so also through Christ our comfort overflows (2 Corinthians 1:5).

I want to know Christ and the power of His resurrection and the fellowship of sharing in His sufferings, becoming like Him in His death, and so, somehow, to attain to the resurrection from the dead (Philippians 3:10).

Dear friends, do not be surprised at the painful trial you are suffering, as though something strange were happening to you. But rejoice that you participate in the sufferings of Christ, so that you may be overjoyed when His glory is revealed (1 Peter 4:12-13).

This does not mean to go looking for suffering and sacrifice just to say that we are now truly worshiping. No, if we live our lives by faith in Jesus—in surrender, submission, servanthood, and selflessness to God—then suffering and sacrifice will come to us. It is strange because you would think that the world would love and praise such qualities, but the world hates them.

So, the apostle Paul asks us to worship by laying down our lives for God. Romans 12:1 says, *"Therefore, I urge you, brothers, in view of God's mercy, to offer your bodies as living sacrifices, holy and pleasing to God—this is your spiritual act of worship."* This is our wonderful privilege in participating in perfect worship of Jesus—submission and sacrifice working together in our lives by the grace of God.

This is "in view of God's mercy." In other words, we lay down our lives in light of the fact that we already have favor with God through Jesus Christ. We are not doing so to try to gain a place of favor with God through sacrificial living and giving. Neither are we doing so to try to bring perfection to a worship already perfect in its quality. We are simply participating in God's grand purpose to bring Jesus' perfect worship to its fullness.

The Cross is worship and worship is the Cross. If submission says, "Here is my will," then sacrifice says, "Here is my life." All of this is present in that one short phrase of Revelation 5:6: *"Then I saw a Lamb, looking as if it had been slain...."* The perfect Lamb brings the perfect sacrifice, which perfects worship for all of us who receive it by faith, for all time.

The Final Paradox of Heavenly Worship

This truth leads us to the final paradox of heavenly worship. All the songs of Revelation 4 and 5 are described in the present; they are happening as John watches and listens. The pinnacle of heavenly worship, however, appears in the past tense and has already happened: *"Then I saw a Lamb, looking as if it had been slain...."* Not only has that sacrifice already happened, but it didn't happen in Heaven either. The greatest act of heavenly worship did not occur in the realm of Heaven and eternity, but was offered up on earth in its linear time and space.

Once a year, the Jewish high priest would perform a sacrifice. He would then bring blood from that sacrifice into the temple's Most Holy Place, offer it on behalf of the people, and sprinkle the blood on the mercy seat. When Jesus died on the Cross outside Jerusalem, He entered the hereafter itself and sprinkled Heaven's mercy seat with His own blood. This was not an eternal act—in the sense of having to happen perpetually—but it was a single act in time with eternal consequences. Such is the argument of Hebrews 9:

> *Then Christ would have had to suffer many times since the creation of the world. But now He has appeared once for all at the end of the ages to do away with sin by the sacrifice of Himself. Just as man is destined to die once, and after that to face judgment, so Christ was sacrificed once to take away the sins of many people* (Hebrews 9:26-28).

Our understanding that the Cross had an immediate effect in Heaven is brought home by the fact that after Jesus' last loud cry and final breath, *"the curtain of the temple was torn in two from top to bottom"* (Mark 15:38). That was a sign to mankind that Jesus had entered Heaven itself as our great High Priest and had sprinkled His blood on the altar for us. Thus, He opened the way for us to come into the Most Holy Presence of our Most Holy God. One act on earth, as done in time and space, allowed God in Christ to reconcile *"to Himself all things, whether things on earth or things in heaven, by making peace through His blood, shed on the cross"* (Col. 1:20). Jesus' perfect act of worship perfected praise in Heaven and earth once and for all.

Understanding this point is important because it has huge implications for our worship. In one sense, the greatest act of heavenly worship did not happen in Heaven at all, but on a trash heap outside of the City of Jerusalem. It happened in the uncertainty and fragility of time and space, not in an unchanging eternity. This act—initiated by God, but fulfilled through the submission of a man, Christ Jesus— took place in the context of terrible sin and darkness, rather than in Heaven's glorious purity and light.

You would have thought that the greatest act of worship must take place in perfect surroundings, with everything in order and just as it should be. The exact opposite is the case: The most perfect act of worship came out of the most carnal, unjust, and wanton act of treacherous violence ever committed in all of God's creation. Satan did the worst that he could do, and so did mankind. Yet, God turned it all into the best worship ever heard in the courts of Heaven. Such is God's total, overwhelming, sovereign power, and such is the unashamed joy and satisfaction that He draws for Himself from the worst of situations.

If satan, who hates the worship of God more than anything else, understood this principle—that God always turns the worst of the devil's devices into the most glorious worship—then he would have stopped tempting and persecuting the saints long ago. He certainly would never martyr anyone ever again. His vain attempts to reduce worship only increases it. Like pouring water on burning oil, he only spreads glorious worship farther and higher.

The point is that Jesus had no opportunity to offer such heavenly worship while still fully God and sitting in the purity and security of Heaven. He had to come to earth and live amongst sin and suffering—as full man and full God—and daily choose to submit and sacrifice. If there had been no temptation to sin on earth, no submission and no sacrifice for Christ, then there would have been no opportunity to offer the greatest ever act of heavenly worship.

This begs the question: Where will our greatest worship be offered—in Heaven or on earth? Without meditating further on these Scriptures, my answer would have been, "In Heaven, of course. That's where we will be perfect and, therefore, able to offer perfect praise." But Jesus had to come to earth to offer His perfect worship. Think about this: If submission and sacrifice are ingredients of the greatest act of heavenly worship, how can that ever be fully realized in an atmosphere without sin or suffering?

During our brief life on earth, we can do parts of worship that we can never do again in all eternity. In Heaven, we will have no further opportunity to sacrifice, or to participate in Christ's sufferings, or to turn to God in our pain, or to turn away from sin. Every choice on earth is an opportunity to worship; every situation and circumstance is an opportunity to offer praise. We will never have those sorts of opportunities again.

Music and songs may be vehicles for the highest form of worship in eternity, but only because there are no more opportunities to lay down a life in adoration of the King. Of course, I am not saying that eternal worship in Heaven is second-class. What I am saying is that we don't have to wait until Heaven before offering heavenly worship. Nor do we have an excuse for living half-hearted lives while on earth, in the belief that we can make up for our poverty of earthly worship in eternity. By the time we get to Heaven, we may have already missed some of our greatest opportunities to worship.

The Lamb's scars will remain, but ours will be gone. In that sense, His sacrificial worship is eternally seen. We, on the other hand, have a window in this life to participate with Jesus in sacrificial worship. Then, that window will vanish into what will be, for us, an eternity without scars.

The songwriter and psalmist Brian Doerksen writes, "Now is the time to worship." How right he is. Now is the time! Whatever we offer, if it is done through faith in Jesus' perfect worship, then it will be received as perfect heavenly worship before Heaven's throne. We do not have to wait for a perfect heart, a perfect voice, or perfect songs. We can offer perfect heavenly worship now because heavenly worship is perfected on earth!

And so Jesus also suffered outside the city gate [in our sinful and broken world] *to make the people holy through His own blood. Let us, then, go to Him outside the camp* [while we are in our sinful and broken world], *bearing the disgrace He bore. For here we do not have an enduring city, but we are looking for the city that is to come* [heaven is coming, but let's not put heavenly worship on hold till then...]. *Through Jesus, therefore, let us continually offer to God a sacrifice of praise* [while we have the opportunity to do it in our sinful and broken world—for it will not be a sacrifice of praise if it is does not include some measure of suffering]—*the fruit of lips that confess His name* (Hebrews 13:12-15).

TO HIM WHO SITS UPON THE THRONE AND TO THE LAMB
BE PRAISE AND HONOR AND GLORY AND POWER,
FOR EVER AND EVER!

(Revelation 5:13)

Books to help you grow strong in Jesus